THE NEW FOLGER LIBRARY SHAKESPEARE

Designed to make Shakespeare's great plays available to all readers, the New Folger Library edition of Shakespeare's plays provides accurate texts in modern spelling and punctuation, as well as scene-by-scene action summaries, full explanatory notes, many pictures clarifying Shakespeare's language, and notes recording all significant departures from the early printed versions. Each play is prefaced by a brief introduction, by a guide to reading Shakespeare's language, and by accounts of his life and theater. Each play is followed by an annotated list of further readings and by a "Modern Perspective" written by an expert on that particular play.

Barbara A. Mowat is Director of Academic Programs at the Folger Shakespeare Library, Executive Editor of *Shakespeare Quarterly*, Chair of the Folger Institute, and author of *The Dramaturgy of Shakespeare's Romances* and of essays on Shakespeare's plays and on the editing of the plays.

Paul Werstine is Professor of English at the Graduate School and at King's University College at the University of Western Ontario. He is general editor of the New Variorum Shakespeare and author of many papers and articles on the printing and editing of Shakespeare's plays.

The Folger Shakespeare Library

The Folger Shakespeare Library in Washington, D.C., a privately funded research library dedicated to Shakespeare and the civilization of early modern Europe, was founded in 1932 by Henry Clay and Emily Jordan Folger. In addition to its role as the world's preeminent Shakespeare collection and its emergence as a leading center for Renaissance studies, the Folger Library offers a wide array of cultural and educational programs and services for the general public.

EDITORS

BARBARA A. MOWAT
Director of Academic Programs
Folger Shakespeare Library

PAUL WERSTINE
Professor of English
King's University College at the University of
Western Ontario, Canada

FOLGER SHAKESPEARE LIBRARY

Twelfth Night, or, What You Will

By
WILLIAM SHAKESPEARE

EDITED BY BARBARA A. MOWAT
AND PAUL WERSTINE

WSP

WASHINGTON SQUARE PRESS
New York   London   Toronto   Sydney

The sale of this book without its cover is unauthorized. If you purchased this book without a cover, you should be aware that it was reported to the publisher as "unsold and destroyed." Neither the author nor the publisher has received payment for the sale of this "stripped book."

A WASHINGTON SQUARE PRESS *Original* Publication

WSP

Washington Square Press
1230 Avenue of the Americas
New York, NY 10020

Copyright © 1993 by The Folger Shakespeare Library

All rights reserved, including the right to reproduce this book or portions thereof in any form whatsoever. For information address Washington Square Press, 1230 Avenue of the Americas, New York, NY 10020

ISBN 13: 978-0-7434-8277-6
ISBN 10:   0-7434-8277-8

Washington Square Press New Folger Edition October 1993
This Edition July 2004

10 9 8

WASHINGTON SQUARE PRESS and colophon are registered trademarks of Simon & Schuster, Inc.

Manufactured in the United States of America

For information regarding special discounts for bulk purchases, please contact Simon & Schuster Special Sales at 1-800-456-6798 or business@simonandschuster.com.

From the Director of the Library

For over four decades, the Folger Library General Reader's Shakespeare provided accurate and accessible texts of the plays and poems to students, teachers, and millions of other interested readers. Today, in an age often impatient with the past, the passion for Shakespeare continues to grow. No author speaks more powerfully to the human condition, in all its variety, than this actor/playwright from a minor sixteenth-century English village.

Over the years vast changes have occurred in the way Shakespeare's works are edited, performed, studied, and taught. The New Folger Library Shakespeare replaces the earlier versions, bringing to bear the best and most current thinking concerning both the texts and their interpretation. Here is an edition which makes the plays and poems fully understandable for modern readers using uncompromising scholarship. Professors Barbara Mowat and Paul Werstine are uniquely qualified to produce this New Folger Shakespeare for a new generation of readers. The Library is grateful for the learning, clarity, and imagination they have brought to this ambitious project.

        Werner Gundersheimer,
        Director of the Folger Shakespeare Library
        from 1984 to 2002

Contents

Editors' Preface	*ix*
Shakespeare's *Twelfth Night, or, What You Will*	*xiii*
Reading Shakespeare's Language	*xiv*
Shakespeare's Life	*xxvi*
Shakespeare's Theater	*xxxiv*
The Publication of Shakespeare's Plays	*xliii*
An Introduction to This Text	*xlvii*
Twelfth Night, or, What You Will	
Text of the Play with Commentary	*1*
Textual Notes	*191*
Twelfth Night: A Modern Perspective	
by Catherine Belsey	*197*
Further Reading	*209*
Key to Famous Lines and Phrases	*221*

Editors' Preface

In recent years, ways of dealing with Shakespeare's texts and with the interpretation of his plays have been undergoing significant change. This edition, while retaining many of the features that have always made the Folger Shakespeare so attractive to the general reader, at the same time reflects these current ways of thinking about Shakespeare. For example, modern readers, actors, and teachers have become interested in the differences between, on the one hand, the early forms in which Shakespeare's plays were first published and, on the other hand, the forms in which editors through the centuries have presented them. In response to this interest, we have based our edition on what we consider the best early printed version of a particular play (explaining our rationale in a section called "An Introduction to This Text") and have marked our changes in the text—unobtrusively, we hope, but in such a way that the curious reader can be aware that a change has been made and can consult the "Textual Notes" to discover what appeared in the early printed version.

Current ways of looking at the plays are reflected in our brief introductions, in many of the commentary notes, in the annotated lists of "Further Reading," and especially in each play's "Modern Perspective," an essay written by an outstanding scholar who brings to the reader his or her fresh assessment of the play in the light of today's interests and concerns.

As in the Folger Library General Reader's Shakespeare, which this edition replaces, we include explanatory notes designed to help make Shakespeare's language clearer to a modern reader, and we place the

ix

notes on the page facing the text that they explain. We also follow the earlier edition in including illustrations —of objects, of clothing, of mythological figures—from books and manuscripts in the Folger Library collection. We provide fresh accounts of the life of Shakespeare, of the publishing of his plays, and of the theaters in which his plays were performed, as well as an introduction to the text itself. We also include a section called "Reading Shakespeare's Language," in which we try to help readers learn to "break the code" of Elizabethan poetic language.

For each section of each volume, we are indebted to a host of generous experts and fellow scholars. The "Reading Shakespeare's Language" sections, for example, could not have been written had not Arthur King, of Brigham Young University, and Randal Robinson, author of *Unlocking Shakespeare's Language*, led the way in untangling Shakespearean language puzzles and shared their insights and methodologies generously with us. "Shakespeare's Life" profited by the careful reading given it by S. Schoenbaum, "Shakespeare's Theater" was read and strengthened by Andrew Gurr and John Astington, and "The Publication of Shakespeare's Plays" is indebted to the comments of Peter W. M. Blayney. We, as editors, take sole responsibility for any errors in our editions.

We are grateful to the authors of the "Modern Perspectives," to Leeds Barroll and David Bevington for their generous encouragement, to the Huntington and Newberry Libraries for fellowship support, to King's College for the grants it has provided to Paul Werstine, to the Social Sciences and Humanities Research Council of Canada, which provided him with a Research Time Stipend for 1990–91, and to the Folger Institute's Center for Shakespeare Studies for its fortuitous sponsorship of a workshop on "Shakespeare's Texts for Students and

Editors' Preface

Teachers" (funded by the National Endowment for the Humanities and led by Richard Knowles of the University of Wisconsin), a workshop from which we learned an enormous amount about what is wanted by college and high-school teachers of Shakespeare today.

Our biggest debt is to the Folger Shakespeare Library: to Werner Gundersheimer, Director of the Library, who has made possible our edition; to Jean Miller, the Library's Art Curator, who combed the Library holdings for illustrations, and to Julie Ainsworth, Head of the Photography Department, who carefully photographed them; to Georgianna Ziegler, Reference Librarian, whose research skills have been invaluable; to Peggy O'Brien, Director of Education, who gave us expert advice about the needs being expressed by Shakespeare teachers and students (and to Martha Christian and other "master teachers" who used our texts in manuscript in their classrooms); to the staff of the Academic Programs Division, especially Paul Menzer (who drafted "Further Reading" material), Mary Tonkinson, Lena Cowen Orlin, Molly Haws, Amy Adler, and Jessica Hymowitz; to Rachel Duchak, who helped us find the "new map"; and, finally, to the staff of the Library Reading Room, whose patience and support have been invaluable.

Barbara A. Mowat and Paul Werstine

Shakespeare's
Twelfth Night, or, What You Will

In *Twelfth Night*, Shakespeare plays with the intersections of love and power. The Countess Olivia is presented to us at the play's beginning as an independent and powerful woman. The sudden deaths of her father and her brother have left her in charge of her own household and have thereby given her power over such male relatives as Sir Toby Belch. Her status as a wealthy, aristocratic single woman makes her the focus of male attention, and she is especially attractive to Duke (or Count) Orsino, who, as the play begins, is already pursuing her. There also circle about her two other would-be suitors: the pretentious and socially ambitious steward, Malvolio, a man whose ambitions make him vulnerable to manipulation by members of Olivia's household; and the weak and foolish Sir Andrew Aguecheek, who is altogether ignored by Olivia but whose delusions of possible marriage to her make him an easy victim of the flattering and swindling Sir Toby.

Onto this scene arrive the well-born twins Viola and Sebastian, and the love of power gives way to the power of love. The twins have been shipwrecked; each thinks the other is drowned; both are destitute. Without protection, Viola chooses to disguise herself as a page, call herself Cesario, and enter into the service of Orsino. In her role as the young Cesario, such is her beauty and her command of language that she immediately wins Orsino's complete trust; he enlists her as his envoy to his beloved Olivia—only to have Olivia fall desperately in love with the beautiful young messenger. Sebastian, too, although without either power or wealth, is similarly irresistible. Antonio, for example, not only saves him from death in the sea but also risks his own life to remain in Sebastian's company.

As is usual in comedy, the play complicates these tangled relationships before it finally and wonderfully untangles them. The title of the play suggests that there is a certain urgency to the need for this disentangling. "Twelfth Night" is the twelfth night after Christmas, the last night of what used to be the extended period of celebration of the Christmas season. Thus it marks the boundary between the time for games and disguisings and the business of the workaday world. The second part of the title, "What You Will," suggests that this play gives us a world that we would all choose (or "will") to enjoy, if we but could.

After you have read the play, we invite you to read "A Modern Perspective" on *Twelfth Night* written by Professor Catherine Belsey of Cardiff University, printed at the back of this book.

Reading Shakespeare's Language

For many people today, reading Shakespeare's language can be a problem—but it is a problem that can be solved. Those who have studied Latin (or even French or German or Spanish), and those who are used to reading poetry, will have little difficulty understanding the language of Shakespeare's poetic drama. Others, though, need to develop the skills of untangling unusual sentence structures and of recognizing and understanding poetic compressions, omissions, and wordplay. And even those skilled in reading unusual sentence structures may have occasional trouble with Shakespeare's words. Four hundred years of "static" intervene between his speaking and our hearing. Most of his immense vocabulary is still in use, but a few of his words are not, and, worse, some of his words now have meanings quite different from those they had in the sixteenth century. In the theater, most of these difficulties are solved for us by actors who study the language and articulate it for us so that the essential meaning is heard—or, when combined with stage action, is at least *felt*. When reading on one's own, one must do what each actor does: go over the lines (often with a dictionary close at hand) until the puzzles are solved and the lines yield up their poetry and the characters speak in words and phrases that are, suddenly, rewarding and wonderfully memorable.

Shakespeare's Words

As you begin to read the opening scenes of a play by Shakespeare, you may notice occasional unfamiliar words. Some are unfamiliar simply because we no longer use them. In the opening scenes of *Twelfth Night*, for example, you will find the words *coistrel* (i.e., a low-born contemptible fellow), *gust* (i.e., taste), *an* (i.e., if), *barful* (i.e., filled with obstacles or barriers), and *indue* (i.e., endow, bestow upon). Words of this kind are explained in notes to the text and will become familiar the more of Shakespeare's plays you read.

In *Twelfth Night*, as in all of Shakespeare's writing, more problematic are the words that we still use but that we use with a different meaning. In the opening scenes of *Twelfth Night*, for example, the word *validity* has the meaning of "worth," *pitch* is used where we would say "excellence," *fell* is used where we would say "fierce" or "deadly," *driving* where we would say "drifting," and *surprise* where we would say "overcome, capture." Such words will be explained in the notes to the text, but they, too, will become familiar as you continue to read Shakespeare's language.

Some words are strange not because of the "static" introduced by changes in language over the past centuries but because these are words that Shakespeare is using to build a dramatic world that has its own space, time, history, and background mythology. In *Twelfth Night*, within the larger world that Shakespeare calls Illyria, he uses one set of words to create the court of Duke Orsino and a second to create the estate of the Lady Olivia. The language that constructs Orsino's world is the language of romantic love as seen in religious and mythological terms. In this world, the beloved is referred to as a "cloistress," her tears are called "eye-offending brine," and her lady-in-waiting is her "handmaid"; the lover, Orsino, portrays himself as the mythological figure Acteon struck down by the "fell and cruel hounds" of his desires, and he prays that his beloved be wounded by the love-god Cupid's "rich golden shaft" so that the "sovereign thrones" of her being will be filled with love for him, her "one self king."

In contrast, the language that creates the world of the Lady Olivia's estate is that of drunken uncles, foolish suitors, clever ladies-in-waiting, and self-important butlers; it is a world of "ducats," "viol-de-gamboys," "substractors," "wenches," "shrews," "buttery bars," cups of "canary," "kickshawses," "jigs," and "galliards." This second, prosaic world is transformed whenever Viola enters Olivia's estate, bringing with her Orsino's petition for Olivia's love and with it language in which love is "divinity" and its songs are "loyal cantons of contemnèd

Reading Shakespeare's Language xvii

love." These language worlds together create the Illyria that Orsino, Olivia, Viola, Sebastian, and their servants and relatives inhabit. The words that create these worlds will become increasingly familiar to you as you read further into the play.

Shakespeare's Sentences

In an English sentence, meaning is quite dependent on the place given each word. "The dog bit the boy" and "The boy bit the dog" mean very different things, even though the individual words are the same. Because English places such importance on the positions of words in sentences, on the way words are arranged, unusual arrangements can puzzle a reader. Shakespeare frequently shifts his sentences away from "normal" English arrangements—often to create the rhythm he seeks, sometimes to use a line's poetic rhythm to emphasize a particular word, sometimes to give a character his or her own speech patterns or to allow the character to speak in a special way. When we attend a good performance of the play, the actors will have worked out the sentence structures and will articulate the sentences so that the meaning is clear. In reading for yourself, do as the actor does. That is, when you become puzzled by a character's speech, check to see if words are being presented in an unusual sequence.

Look first for the placement of subject and verb. Shakespeare often places the verb before the subject (e.g., instead of "He goes" we find "Goes he"). In *Twelfth Night*, we find such a construction in Orsino's "O spirit of love, how quick and fresh *art thou*," as well as in the Captain's "*Be you* his eunuch" and in Toby's "Then *hadst thou had* an excellent head of hair" (instead of "thou hadst had . . ."). Orsino's "That instant *was I* turned into a hart" is another example of inverted subject and verb.

Such inversions rarely cause much confusion. More problematic is Shakespeare's frequent placing of the object or the predicate adjective before the subject and verb (e.g., instead of "I hit him," we might find "Him I hit," or, instead of "It is black," we might find "Black it is"). Viola's "What else may hap, to time I will commit" is an example of such an inversion (the normal order would be "I will commit what else may hap [i.e., whatever else may happen] to time"). Another example is Orsino's "So full of shapes is fancy," where the phrase serving as predicate adjective ("so full of shapes") precedes the subject and verb, and where the subject and verb are themselves inverted. (The normal order would be "Fancy is so full of shapes.")

Inversions are not the only unusual sentence structures in Shakespeare's language. Often in his sentences words that would normally appear together are separated from each other. (Again, this is often done to create a particular rhythm or to stress a particular word.) Take, for example, Orsino's "when liver, brain, and heart, / These sovereign thrones, are all supplied, and filled / Her sweet perfections with one self king"; here the phrase "These sovereign thrones" separates the subject ("liver, brain, and heart") from its verb ("are"), and the phrase "Her sweet perfections" interrupts the phrase "filled with." Or take the Captain's lines: "And then 'twas fresh in murmur (as, you know, / What great ones do the less will prattle of) / That he did seek the love of fair Olivia," where the normal construction "'twas fresh in murmur that he did seek the love of fair Olivia" is interrupted by the insertion of the parenthetical "as, you know, what great ones do the less will prattle of." In order to create for yourself sentences that seem more like the English of everyday speech, you may wish to rearrange the words, putting together the word clusters ("liver, brain, and heart are," "Her sweet perfections filled with," "'twas fresh in murmur that"). You will usually find that the sentence will gain in clarity but will lose its rhythm or shift its emphasis.

Locating and rearranging words that "belong together" is especially necessary in passages that separate basic sentence elements by long delaying or expanding interruptions. When the Captain tells Viola about his last sight of her brother Sebastian ("I saw your brother bind himself to a strong mast, where I saw him hold acquaintance with the waves so long as I could see"), he uses a construction that both delays the main sentence elements until subordinate material is presented and then interrupts the sentence elements with additional subordinate material:

Assure yourself, after our ship did split,
When you and those poor number saved with you
Hung on our driving boat, *I saw your brother*,
Most provident in peril, *bind himself*
(Courage and hope both teaching him the practice)
To a strong mast that lived upon the sea,
Where, like Arion on the dolphin's back,
I saw him hold acquaintance with the waves
So long as I could see.

In some of Shakespeare's plays (*Hamlet*, for instance), long interrupted sentences and sentences in which the basic sentence elements are significantly delayed are used frequently, sometimes to catch the audience up in the narrative and sometimes as a characterizing device. They appear rarely in *Twelfth Night*, where sentences tend to be structurally straightforward.

Finally, in many of Shakespeare's plays, sentences are sometimes complicated not because of unusual structures or interruptions but because Shakespeare omits words and parts of words that English sentences normally require. (In conversation, we, too, often omit words. We say "Heard from him yet?" and our hearer supplies the missing "Have you.") Frequent reading of Shakespeare—and of other poets—trains us to supply such missing words. In some plays, Shakespeare uses omissions both of verbs and of nouns to great dramatic effect. In *Twelfth Night* omissions are rare and seem to be used to affect the tone of the speech or for the sake of speech rhythm. For example, Sir Andrew's "I'll home tomorrow" (where "go" is omitted) lends a colloquial flavor to his speech, and Orsino's "I myself am best / When least in company" (where "I am" is omitted before "least") creates a regular iambic pentameter line.

Shakespearean Wordplay

Shakespeare plays with language so often and so variously that entire books are written on the topic. Here we will mention only two kinds of wordplay, puns and metaphors. A pun is a play on words that sound the same but that have different meanings (or on a single word that has more than one meaning). In the opening scene of *Twelfth Night*, a pun on the words *heart* and *hart* underlies this exchange between Orsino and Curio: "Will you go hunt, my lord?" "What, Curio?" "The hart." "Why, so I do, the noblest that I have." In a later scene Olivia, curious about the "man" who refuses to leave the gate of her estate, asks "What manner [i.e., kind] of man" he is. Malvolio's response, "Of very ill manner," puns on the word *manner*, using its meaning of "behavior." In this exchange between Maria and the Fool—

FOOL ... I am resolved on two points.
MARIA That if one break, the other will hold, or, if both break, your gaskins fall—

Maria puns on the word *points*, which meant not only the "points" of an argument but also the laces that held up a man's breeches.

Because of the presence of the Fool, who makes his living by using wordplay to amuse his aristocratic patron and others in the household, *Twelfth Night* is among Shakespeare's plays that use puns frequently. The Fool's opening exchange with Olivia in Act 1, scene 5—an exchange that succeeds in amusing her and thus saving the Fool's threatened position in the household—turns on his successful play on the word *Fool* (the name given the profession he follows) and *fool* (a person who behaves foolishly). Within this larger exchange, Olivia calls him a "dry [i.e., dull, not amusing] Fool" who has grown "dishonest"; his defense is a series of puns: "give the dry [i.e., dull] Fool drink, then is the Fool not dry [i.e., thirsty]. Bid the dishonest man mend [i.e., (1) reform, (2) repair] himself; if he mend [i.e., reform], he is no longer dishonest; if he cannot, let the botcher [i.e., tailor who repairs clothing] mend [i.e., repair] him." Such puns characterize the Fool's "foolery"—so much so that the language in this play, and the Fool's language in particular, needs to be listened to carefully if one is to catch all its meanings.

A metaphor is a play on words in which one object or idea is expressed as if it were something else, something with which it shares common features. In the opening lines of *Twelfth Night*—

> If music be the food of love, play on.
> Give me excess of it, that, surfeiting,
> The appetite may sicken and so die—

metaphoric language is used to express the longings of love as a physical hunger for which music is a satisfying food. As a way of saying that he wishes he were not so much in love, Orsino asks that his love be given an excessive amount of music so that love's appetite will be killed by overeating. A few lines later Orsino uses another metaphor to express the intensity of his love:

> O, when mine eyes did see Olivia first,
> . . . . .
> That instant was I turned into a hart,
> And my desires, like fell and cruel hounds,
> E'er since pursue me.

Here the lover, having seen his beloved, is pursued by his desires like a deer by hunting dogs. (Shakespeare's audience would have recognized behind this metaphor the famous mythological account of the hunter Acteon, who, having seen the goddess Diana naked, was literally turned into a deer and destroyed by his own hounds.)

Later in the play (in 3.1) Olivia uses metaphor to express her own love pains. Having fallen in love with Cesario, she has, she thinks, earned his scorn by sending a ring to him. "What might you think?" she asks.

> Have you not set mine honor at the stake,
> And baited it with all th' unmuzzled thoughts
> That tyrannous heart can think?

In this metaphor, her honor is like a bear tied to the stake and attacked by the vicious dogs of Cesario's harsh thoughts.

In *Twelfth Night* one occasionally finds metaphor used to control long stretches of dialogue. In Act 1, scene 5, Viola/Cesario addresses Olivia with the claim that his message is, to Olivia's ears, divinity (i.e., something holy). Olivia responds as if "divinity" meant "theology," and asks for Cesario's "text" (i.e., the scriptural passage on which he is to expound). Olivia thus sets up a metaphor that continues for several lines of dialogue through the words *doctrine, chapter, method, the first,* and *heresy:*

VIOLA The rudeness that hath appeared in me have I learned from my entertainment. What I am and what I would are as secret as maidenhead: to your ears, divinity; to any other's, profanation.
OLIVIA Give us the place alone. We will hear this divinity. (*Maria and Attendants exit.*) Now, sir, what is your text?
VIOLA Most sweet lady—
OLIVIA A comfortable doctrine, and much may be said of it. Where lies your text?
VIOLA In Orsino's bosom.
OLIVIA In his bosom? In what chapter of his bosom?
VIOLA To answer by the method, in the first of his heart.
OLIVIA O, I have read it; it is heresy. Have you no more to say?
VIOLA Good madam, let me see your face.
OLIVIA Have you any commission from your lord to negotiate with my face? You are now out of your text. But we will draw the curtain and show you the picture. (*She removes her veil.*)

With Olivia's "we will draw the curtain and show you the picture," the controlling metaphor shifts from "love message as sermon" to "veiled face as covered portrait," a metaphor that progresses through Olivia's "such a one I was this present" through "'Tis in grain" and "'Tis beauty truly blent."

In most of Shakespeare's plays, metaphors are most

often used when the idea being conveyed seems hard to express, and the speaker is thus given language that helps to carry the idea or the feeling to his or her listener—and to the audience. In *Romeo and Juliet,* for example, Romeo's metaphors of Juliet-as-saint and Juliet-as-light employ images from the poetic tradition that seem designed to portray a lover struggling to express the overpowering feelings that come with being in love. In *Twelfth Night* one senses that metaphors are to be heard not so much as sincere attempts to express deep feelings as they are a playing with language, a deliberate heightening of emotion for self-indulgence or for display.

Implied Stage Action

Finally, in reading Shakespeare's plays we should always remember that what we are reading is a performance script. The dialogue is written to be spoken by actors who, at the same time, are moving, gesturing, picking up objects, weeping, shaking their fists. Some stage action is described in what are called "stage directions"; some is suggested within the dialogue itself. Learn to be alert to such signals as you stage the play in your imagination. When, in *Twelfth Night,* Sir Andrew says to Maria "Here's my hand," and a few lines later she says to him "Now I let go your hand," it is clear what stage action has occurred. Again, when, at the end of Act 1, scene 3, Sir Toby says to Sir Andrew "Let me see thee caper. Ha, higher! Ha, ha, excellent!" one knows that Sir Andrew at least attempts to dance a lively dance. At several places in *Twelfth Night,* signals to the reader are not quite so clear. When, after Olivia's first meeting with Cesario, Malvolio says to Cesario "She returns this ring to you. . . . Receive it so. . . . you peevishly threw it to her, and her will is it should be so returned. If it be worth stooping for, there it lies . . . ," one assumes that, at some point during these speeches, Malvolio throws down the ring; one assumes, also, that Viola/Cesario picks up the ring at some point during her speech after Malvolio exits. But the stage action in this scene is not clearly prescribed in the dialogue and must be decided upon by the actors, by the reader, or by editors who, as in the case of this edition, choose to add stage directions.

More demanding for the director and the actors (and for the reader, in imagination) is the stage action of 3.4, where many bits of stage business—both in the attempts to get Viola/Cesario and Sir Andrew to fight, and in the fight between Antonio and Sir Toby and in Antonio's arrest—may be played variously from production to production. Learning to read the language of stage action repays one many times over when one reaches a scene like that of the gulling of Malvolio (2.5) or the play's final scene, with its succession of entrances and exits climaxing in the breathtaking entrance of Sebastian.

It is immensely rewarding to work carefully with Shakespeare's language so that the words, the sentences, the wordplay, and the implied stage action all become clear—as readers for the past four centuries have discovered. It may be more pleasurable to attend a good performance of a play—though not everyone has thought so. But the joy of being able to stage one of Shakespeare's plays in one's imagination, to return to passages that continue to yield further meanings (or further questions) the more one reads them—these are pleasures that, for many, rival (or at least augment) those of the performed text, and certainly make it worth considerable effort to "break the code" of Elizabethan poetic drama and let free the remarkable language that makes up a Shakespeare text.

Shakespeare's Life

Surviving documents that give us glimpses into the life of William Shakespeare show us a playwright, poet, and actor who grew up in the market town of Stratford-upon-Avon, spent his professional life in London, and returned to Stratford a wealthy landowner. He was born in April 1564, died in April 1616, and is buried inside the chancel of Holy Trinity Church in Stratford.

We wish we could know more about the life of the world's greatest dramatist. His plays and poems are testaments to his wide reading—especially to his knowledge of Virgil, Ovid, Plutarch, Holinshed's *Chronicles*, and the Bible—and to his mastery of the English language, but we can only speculate about his education. We know that the King's New School in Stratford-upon-Avon was considered excellent. The school was one of the English "grammar schools" established to educate young men, primarily in Latin grammar and literature. As in other schools of the time, students began their studies at the age of four or five in the attached "petty school," and there learned to read and write in English, studying primarily the catechism from the Book of Common Prayer. After two years in the petty school, students entered the lower form (grade) of the grammar school, where they began the serious study of Latin grammar and Latin texts that would occupy most of the remainder of their school days. (Several Latin texts that Shakespeare used repeatedly in writing his plays and poems were texts that schoolboys memorized and recited.) Latin comedies were introduced early in the lower form; in the upper form, which the boys entered at age ten or eleven, students wrote their own Latin orations and declamations, studied Latin historians and rhetoricians, and began the study of Greek using the Greek New Testament.

Since the records of the Stratford "grammar school" do not survive, we cannot prove that William Shakespeare attended the school; however, every indication (his father's position as an alderman and bailiff of Stratford, the playwright's own knowledge of the Latin classics, scenes in the plays that recall grammar-school experiences—for example, *The Merry Wives of Windsor*, 4.1) suggests that he did. We also lack generally accepted documentation about Shakespeare's life after his schooling ended and his professional life in London began. His marriage in 1582 (at age eighteen) to Anne Hathaway and the subsequent births of his daughter Susanna (1583) and the twins Judith and Hamnet (1585) are recorded, but how he supported himself and where he lived are not known. Nor do we know when and why he left Stratford for the London theatrical world, nor how he rose to be the important figure in that world that he had become by the early 1590s.

We do know that by 1592 he had achieved some prominence in London as both an actor and a playwright. In that year was published a book by the playwright Robert Greene attacking an actor who had the audacity to write blank-verse drama and who was "in his own conceit [i.e., opinion] the only Shake-scene in a country." Since Greene's attack includes a parody of a line from one of Shakespeare's early plays, there is little doubt that it is Shakespeare to whom he refers, a "Shake-scene" who had aroused Greene's fury by successfully competing with university-educated dramatists like Greene himself. It was in 1593 that Shakespeare became a published poet. In that year he published his long narrative poem *Venus and Adonis;* in 1594, he followed it with *The Rape of Lucrece*. Both poems were dedicated to the young earl of Southampton

(Henry Wriothesley), who may have become Shakespeare's patron.

It seems no coincidence that Shakespeare wrote these narrative poems at a time when the theaters were closed because of the plague, a contagious epidemic disease that devastated the population of London. When the theaters reopened in 1594, Shakespeare apparently resumed his double career of actor and playwright and began his long (and seemingly profitable) service as an acting-company shareholder. Records for December of 1594 show him to be a leading member of the Lord Chamberlain's Men. It was this company of actors, later named the King's Men, for whom he would be a principal actor, dramatist, and shareholder for the rest of his career.

So far as we can tell, that career spanned about twenty years. In the 1590s, he wrote his plays on English history as well as several comedies and at least two tragedies (*Titus Andronicus* and *Romeo and Juliet*). These histories, comedies, and tragedies are the plays credited to him in 1598 in a work, *Palladis Tamia*, that in one chapter compares English writers with "Greek, Latin, and Italian Poets." There the author, Francis Meres, claims that Shakespeare is comparable to the Latin dramatists Seneca for tragedy and Plautus for comedy, and calls him "the most excellent in both kinds for the stage." He also names him "Mellifluous and honey-tongued Shakespeare": "I say," writes Meres, "that the Muses would speak with Shakespeare's fine filed phrase, if they would speak English." Since Meres also mentions Shakespeare's "sugared sonnets among his private friends," it is assumed that many of Shakespeare's sonnets (not published until 1609) were also written in the 1590s.

In 1599, Shakespeare's company built a theater for themselves across the river from London, naming it the

Globe. The plays that are considered by many to be Shakespeare's major tragedies (*Hamlet, Othello, King Lear,* and *Macbeth*) were written while the company was resident in this theater, as were such comedies as *Twelfth Night* and *Measure for Measure*. Many of Shakespeare's plays were performed at court (both for Queen Elizabeth I and, after her death in 1603, for King James I), some were presented at the Inns of Court (the residences of London's legal societies), and some were doubtless performed in other towns, at the universities, and at great houses when the King's Men went on tour; otherwise, his plays from 1599 to 1608 were, so far as we know, performed only at the Globe. Between 1608 and 1612, Shakespeare wrote several plays—among them *The Winter's Tale* and *The Tempest*—presumably for the company's new indoor Blackfriars theater, though the plays seem to have been performed also at the Globe and at court. Surviving documents describe a performance of *The Winter's Tale* in 1611 at the Globe, for example, and performances of *The Tempest* in 1611 and 1613 at the royal palace of Whitehall.

Shakespeare wrote very little after 1612, the year in which he probably wrote *King Henry VIII*. (It was at a performance of *Henry VIII* in 1613 that the Globe caught fire and burned to the ground.) Sometime between 1610 and 1613 he seems to have returned to live in Stratford-upon-Avon, where he owned a large house and considerable property, and where his wife and his two daughters and their husbands lived. (His son Hamnet had died in 1596.) During his professional years in London, Shakespeare had presumably derived income from the acting company's profits as well as from his own career as an actor, from the sale of his play manuscripts to the acting company, and, after 1599, from his shares as an owner of the Globe. It was presumably that income, carefully invested in land and other property, that made him the wealthy man that surviving documents show him to have become. It is also assumed that William Shakespeare's growing wealth and reputation played some part in inclining the crown, in 1596, to grant John Shakespeare, William's father, the coat of arms that he had so long sought. William Shakespeare died in Stratford on April 23, 1616 (according to the epitaph carved under his bust in Holy Trinity Church) and was buried on April 25. Seven years after his death, his collected plays were published as *Mr. William Shakespeares Comedies, Histories, & Tragedies* (the work now known as the First Folio).

The years in which Shakespeare wrote were among the most exciting in English history. Intellectually, the discovery, translation, and printing of Greek and Roman classics were making available a set of works and worldviews that interacted complexly with Christian texts and beliefs. The result was a questioning, a vital intellectual ferment, that provided energy for the period's amazing dramatic and literary output and that fed directly into Shakespeare's plays. The Ghost in *Hamlet*, for example, is wonderfully complicated in part because he is a figure from Roman tragedy—the spirit of the dead returning to seek revenge—who at the same time inhabits a Christian hell (or purgatory); Hamlet's description of humankind reflects at one moment the Neoplatonic wonderment at mankind ("What a piece of work is a man!") and, at the next, the Christian disparagement of human sinners ("And yet, to me, what is this quintessence of dust?").

As intellectual horizons expanded, so also did geographical and cosmological horizons. New worlds—both North and South America—were explored, and in them were found human beings who lived and worshiped in ways radically different from those of Renaissance Europeans and Englishmen. The universe during

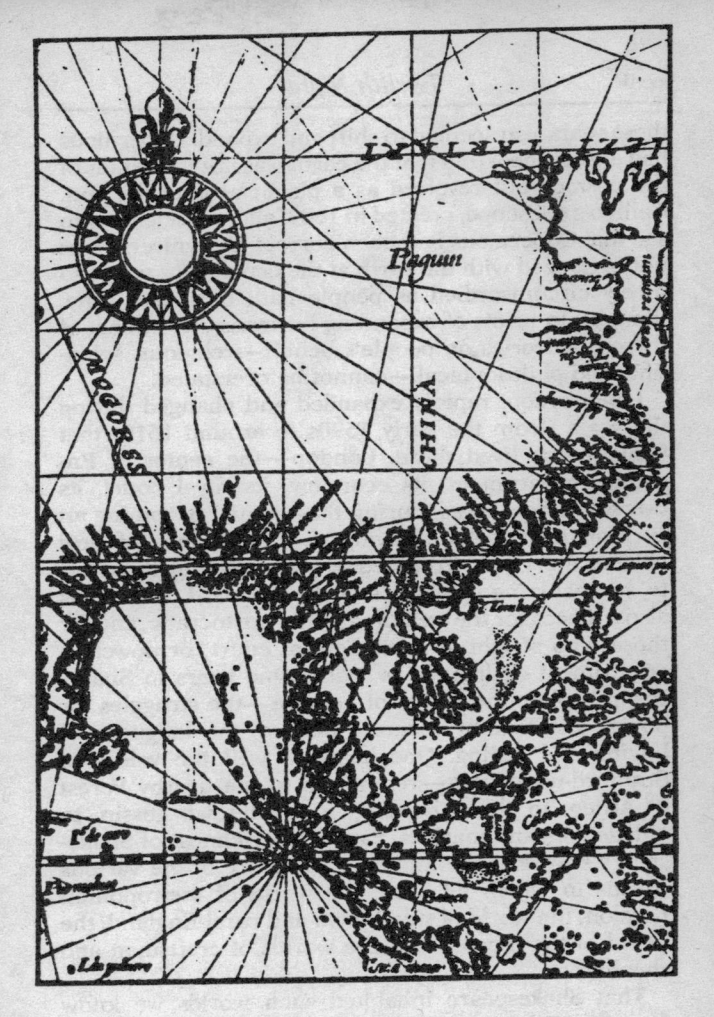

Edward Wright's "new map" of the world with "the augmentation of the Indies" (formerly attributed to E. Molyneux), reproduced for Richard Hakluyt and prefixed to his *Principal navigations*, II (1599). Published by permission of the Map Division of the Library of Congress.

these years also seemed to shift and expand. Copernicus had earlier theorized that the earth was not the center of the cosmos but revolved as a planet around the sun. Galileo's telescope, created in 1609, allowed scientists to see that Copernicus had been correct: the universe was not organized with the earth at the center, nor was it so nicely circumscribed as people had, until that time, thought. In terms of expanding horizons, the impact of these discoveries on people's beliefs—religious, scientific, and philosophical—cannot be overstated.

London, too, rapidly expanded and changed during the years (from the early 1590s to around 1610) that Shakespeare lived there. London—the center of England's government, its economy, its royal court, its overseas trade—was, during these years, becoming an exciting metropolis, drawing to it thousands of new citizens every year. Troubled by overcrowding, by poverty, by recurring epidemics of the plague, London was also a mecca for the wealthy and the aristocratic, and for those who sought advancement at court, or power in government or finance or trade. One hears in Shakespeare's plays the voices of London—the struggles for power, the fear of venereal disease, the language of buying and selling. One hears as well the voices of Stratford-upon-Avon—references to the nearby Forest of Arden; to sheep herding, to small-town gossip, to village fairs and markets. Part of the richness of Shakespeare's work is the influence felt there of the various worlds in which he lived: the world of metropolitan London, the world of small-town and rural England, the world of the theater, and the worlds of craftsmen and shepherds.

That Shakespeare inhabited such worlds we know from surviving London and Stratford documents, as well as from the evidence of the plays and poems themselves. From such records we can sketch the dramatist's life. We know from his works that he was a voracious reader. We know from legal and business documents that he was a multifaceted theater man who became a wealthy landowner. We know a bit about his family life and a fair amount about his legal and financial dealings. Most scholars today depend upon such evidence as they draw their picture of the world's greatest playwright. Such, however, has not always been the case. Until the late eighteenth century, the William Shakespeare who lived in most biographies was the creation of legend and tradition. This was the Shakespeare who was supposedly caught poaching deer at Charlecote, the estate of Sir Thomas Lucy close by Stratford; this was the Shakespeare who fled from Sir Thomas's vengeance and made his way in London by taking care of horses outside a playhouse; this was the Shakespeare who reportedly could barely read, but whose natural gifts were extraordinary, whose father was a butcher who allowed his gifted son sometimes to help in the butcher shop, where William supposedly killed calves "in a high style," making a speech for the occasion. It was this legendary William Shakespeare whose Falstaff (in *1 and 2 Henry IV*) so pleased Queen Elizabeth that she demanded a play about Falstaff in love, and demanded that it be written in fourteen days (hence the existence of *The Merry Wives of Windsor*). It was this legendary Shakespeare who reached the top of his acting career in the roles of the Ghost in *Hamlet* and old Adam in *As You Like It*—and who died of a fever contracted by drinking too hard at "a merry meeting" with the poets Michael Drayton and Ben Jonson. This legendary Shakespeare is a rambunctious, undisciplined man, as attractively "wild" as his plays were seen by earlier generations to be. Unfortunately, there is no trace of evidence to support these wonderful stories.

Perhaps in response to the disreputable Shakespeare

of legend—or perhaps in response to the fragmentary and, for some, all-too-ordinary Shakespeare documented by surviving records—some people since the mid-nineteenth century have argued that William Shakespeare could not have written the plays that bear his name. These persons have put forward some dozen names as more likely authors, among them Queen Elizabeth, Sir Francis Bacon, Edward de Vere (earl of Oxford), and Christopher Marlowe. Such attempts to find what for these people is a more believable author of the plays is a tribute to the regard in which the plays are held. Unfortunately for their claims, the documents that exist that provide evidence for the facts of Shakespeare's life tie him inextricably to the body of plays and poems that bear his name. Unlikely as it seems to those who want the works to have been written by an aristocrat, a university graduate, or an "important" person, the plays and poems seem clearly to have been produced by a man from Stratford-upon-Avon with a very good "grammar-school" education and a life of experience in London and in the world of the London theater. How this particular man produced the works that dominate the cultures of much of the world almost four hundred years after his death is one of life's mysteries—and one that will continue to tease our imaginations as we continue to delight in his plays and poems.

Shakespeare's Theater

The actors of Shakespeare's time are known to have performed plays in a great variety of locations. They played at court (that is, in the great halls of such royal residences as Whitehall, Hampton Court, and Greenwich); they played in halls at the universities of Oxford and Cambridge, and at the Inns of Court (the residences in London of the legal societies); and they also played in the private houses of great lords and civic officials. Sometimes acting companies went on tour from London into the provinces, often (but not only) when outbreaks of bubonic plague in the capital forced the closing of theaters to reduce the possibility of contagion in crowded audiences. In the provinces the actors usually staged their plays in churches (until around 1600) or in guildhalls. While surviving records show only a handful of occasions when actors played at inns while on tour, London inns were important playing places up until the 1590s.

The building of theaters in London had begun only shortly before Shakespeare wrote his first plays in the 1590s. These theaters were of two kinds: outdoor or public playhouses that could accommodate large numbers of playgoers, and indoor or private theaters for much smaller audiences. What is usually regarded as the first London outdoor public playhouse was called simply the Theatre. James Burbage—the father of Richard Burbage, who was perhaps the most famous actor in Shakespeare's company—built it in 1576 in an area north of the city of London called Shoreditch. Among the more famous of the other public playhouses that capitalized on the new fashion were the Curtain and the Fortune (both also built north of the city), the Rose, the Swan, the Globe, and the Hope (all located on the Bankside, a region just across the Thames south of the city of London). All these playhouses had to be built outside the jurisdiction of the city of London because many civic officials were hostile to the performance of drama and repeatedly petitioned the royal council to abolish it.

The theaters erected on the Bankside (a region under

the authority of the Church of England, whose head was the monarch) shared the neighborhood with houses of prostitution and with the Paris Garden, where the blood sports of bearbaiting and bullbaiting were carried on. There may have been no clear distinction between playhouses and buildings for such sports, for we know that the Hope was used for both plays and baiting and that Philip Henslowe, owner of the Rose and, later, partner in the ownership of the Fortune, was also a partner in a monopoly on baiting. All these forms of entertainment were easily accessible to Londoners by boat across the Thames or over London Bridge.

Evidently Shakespeare's company prospered on the Bankside. They moved there in 1599. Threatened by difficulties in renewing the lease on the land where their first theater (the Theatre) had been built, Shakespeare's company took advantage of the Christmas holiday in 1598 to dismantle the Theatre and transport its timbers across the Thames to the Bankside, where, in 1599, these timbers were used in the building of the Globe. The weather in late December 1598 is recorded as having been especially harsh. It was so cold that the Thames was "nigh [nearly] frozen," and there was heavy snow. Perhaps the weather aided Shakespeare's company in eluding their landlord, the snow hiding their activity and the freezing of the Thames allowing them to slide the timbers across to the Bankside without paying tolls for repeated trips over London Bridge. Attractive as this narrative is, it remains just as likely that the heavy snow hampered transport of the timbers in wagons through the London streets to the river. It also must be remembered that the Thames was, according to report, only "nigh frozen" and therefore as impassable as it ever was. Whatever the precise circumstances of this fascinating event in English theater history, Shakespeare's company was able to begin playing at their new Globe theater on the Bankside in 1599. After the first Globe burned down in 1613 during the staging of Shakespeare's *Henry VIII* (its thatch roof was set alight by cannon fire called for by the performance), Shakespeare's company immediately rebuilt on the same location. The second Globe seems to have been a grander structure than its predecessor. It remained in use until the beginning of the English Civil War in 1642, when Parliament officially closed the theaters. Soon thereafter it was pulled down.

The public theaters of Shakespeare's time were very different buildings from our theaters today. First of all, they were open-air playhouses. As recent excavations of the Rose and the Globe confirm, some were polygonal or roughly circular in shape; the Fortune, however, was square. The most recent estimates of their size put the diameter of these buildings at 72 feet (the Rose) to 100 feet (the Globe), but we know that they held vast audiences of two or three thousand, who must have been squeezed together quite tightly. Some of these spectators paid extra to sit or stand in the two or three levels of roofed galleries that extended, on the upper levels, all the way around the theater and surrounded an open space. In this space were the stage and, perhaps, the tiring house (what we would call dressing rooms), as well as the so-called yard. In the yard stood the spectators who chose to pay less, the ones whom Hamlet contemptuously called "groundlings." For a roof they had only the sky, and so they were exposed to all kinds of weather. They stood on a floor that was sometimes made of mortar and sometimes of ash mixed with the shells of hazelnuts. The latter provided a porous and therefore dry footing for the crowd, and the shells may have been more comfortable to stand on because they were not as hard as mortar. Availability of shells may not have been a problem if hazelnuts were a favorite food for Shakespeare's audiences to munch on as they watched his plays. Archaeologists who are today unearthing the remains of theaters from this period have discovered quantities of these nutshells on theater sites.

Unlike the yard, the stage itself was covered by a roof. Its ceiling, called "the heavens," is thought to have been elaborately painted to depict the sun, moon, stars, and planets. Just how big the stage was remains hard to determine. We have a single sketch of part of the interior of the Swan. A Dutchman named Johannes de Witt visited this theater around 1596 and sent a sketch of it back to his friend, Arend van Buchel. Because van Buchel found de Witt's letter and sketch of interest, he copied both into a book. It is van Buchel's copy, adapted, it seems, to the shape and size of the page in his book, that survives. In this sketch, the stage appears to be a large rectangular platform that thrusts far out into the yard, perhaps even as far as the center of the circle formed by the surrounding galleries. This drawing, combined with the specifications for the size of the stage in the building contract for the Fortune, has led scholars to conjecture that the stage on which Shakespeare's plays were performed must have measured approximately 43 feet in width and 27 feet in depth, a vast acting area. But the digging up of a large part of the Rose by archaeologists has provided evidence of a quite different stage design. The Rose stage was a platform tapered at the corners and much shallower than what seems to be depicted in the van Buchel sketch. Indeed, its measurements seem to be about 37.5 feet across at its widest point and only 15.5 feet deep. Because the surviving indications of stage size and design differ from each other so much, it is possible that the stages in other theaters, like the Theatre, the Curtain, and the Globe (the outdoor playhouses where we know that Shakespeare's plays were performed), were different from those at both the Swan and the Rose.

After about 1608 Shakespeare's plays were staged not only at the Globe but also at an indoor or private playhouse in Blackfriars. This theater had been constructed in 1596 by James Burbage in an upper hall of a former Dominican priory or monastic house. Although Henry VIII had dissolved all English monasteries in the 1530s (shortly after he had founded the Church of England), the area remained under church, rather than hostile civic, control. The hall that Burbage had purchased and renovated was a large one in which Parliament had once met. In the private theater that he constructed, the stage, lit by candles, was built across the narrow end of the hall, with boxes flanking it. The rest of the hall offered seating room only. Because there was no provision for standing room, the largest audience it could hold was less than a thousand, or about a quarter of what the Globe could accommodate. Admission to Blackfriars was correspondingly more expensive. Instead of a penny to stand in the yard at the Globe, it cost a minimum of sixpence to get into Blackfriars. The best seats at the Globe (in the Lords' Room in the gallery above and behind the stage) cost sixpence; but the boxes flanking the stage at Blackfriars were half a crown, or five times sixpence. Some spectators who were particularly interested in displaying themselves paid even more to sit on stools on the Blackfriars stage.

Whether in the outdoor or indoor playhouses, the stages of Shakespeare's time were different from ours. They were not separated from the audience by the dropping of a curtain between acts and scenes. Therefore the playwrights of the time had to find other ways of signaling to the audience that one scene (to be imagined as occurring in one location at a given time) had ended and the next (to be imagined at perhaps a different location at a later time) had begun. The customary way used by Shakespeare and many of his contemporaries was to have everyone onstage exit at the end of one scene and have one or more different characters enter to begin the next. In a few cases, where characters remain onstage from one scene to another, the dialogue or stage action makes the change of location clear, and the characters are generally to be imagined as having moved from one place to another. For example, in *Romeo and Juliet*, Romeo and his friends remain onstage in Act 1 from scene 4 to scene 5, but they are represented as having moved between scenes from the street that leads to Capulet's house into Capulet's house itself. The new location is signaled in part by the appearance onstage of Capulet's servingmen carrying napkins, something they would not take into the streets. Playwrights had to be quite resourceful in the use of hand properties, like the napkin, or in the use of dialogue to specify where the action was taking place in their plays because, in contrast to most of today's theaters, the playhouses of Shakespeare's time did not use movable scenery to dress the stage and make the setting precise. As another consequence of this difference, however, the playwrights of Shakespeare's time did not have to specify exactly where the action of their plays was set when they did not choose to do so, and much of the action of their plays is tied to no specific place.

Usually Shakespeare's stage is referred to as a "bare stage," to distinguish it from the stages of the last two or three centuries with their elaborate sets. But the stage in Shakespeare's time was not completely bare. Philip Henslowe, owner of the Rose, lists in his inventory of stage properties a rock, three tombs, and two mossy banks. Stage directions in plays of the time also call for such things as thrones (or "states"), banquets (presumably tables with plaster replicas of food on them), and beds and tombs to be pushed onto the stage. Thus the stage often held more than the actors.

The actors did not limit their performing to the stage alone. Occasionally they went beneath the stage, as the Ghost appears to do in the first act of *Hamlet*. From there they could emerge onto the stage through a trapdoor. They could retire behind the hangings across the back of the stage (or the front of the tiring house), as, for example, the actor playing Polonius does when he hides behind the arras. Sometimes the hangings could be drawn back during a performance to "discover" one or more actors behind them. When performance required that an actor appear "above," as when Juliet is imagined to stand at the window of her chamber in the famous and misnamed "balcony scene," then the actor probably climbed the stairs to the gallery over the back of the stage and temporarily shared it with some of the spectators. The stage was also provided with ropes and winches so that actors could descend from, and reascend to, the "heavens."

Perhaps the greatest difference between dramatic performances in Shakespeare's time and ours was that in Shakespeare's England the roles of women were played by boys. (Some of these boys grew up to take male roles in their maturity.) There were no women in the acting companies, only in the audience. It had not always been so in the history of the English stage. There are records of women on English stages in the thirteenth and fourteenth centuries, two hundred years before Shakespeare's plays were performed. After the accession of James I in 1603, the queen of England and her ladies took part in entertainments at court called masques, and with the reopening of the theaters in 1660 at the restoration of Charles II, women again took their place on the public stage.

The chief competitors for the companies of adult

actors such as the one to which Shakespeare belonged and for which he wrote were companies of exclusively boy actors. The competition was most intense in the early 1600s. There were then two principal children's companies: the Children of Paul's (the choirboys from St. Paul's Cathedral, whose private playhouse was near the cathedral); and the Children of the Chapel Royal (the choirboys from the monarch's private chapel, who performed at the Blackfriars theater built by Burbage in 1596, which Shakespeare's company had been stopped from using by local residents who objected to crowds). In *Hamlet* Shakespeare writes of "an aerie [nest] of children, little eyases [hawks], that cry out on the top of question and are most tyrannically clapped for 't. These are now the fashion and . . . berattle the common stages [attack the public theaters]." In the long run, the adult actors prevailed. The Children of Paul's dissolved around 1606. By about 1608 the Children of the Chapel Royal had been forced to stop playing at the Blackfriars theater, which was then taken over by the King's Men, Shakespeare's own troupe.

Acting companies and theaters of Shakespeare's time were organized in different ways. For example, Philip Henslowe owned the Rose and leased it to companies of actors, who paid him from their takings. Henslowe would act as manager of these companies, initially paying playwrights for their plays and buying properties, recovering his outlay from the actors. Shakespeare's company, however, managed itself, with the principal actors, Shakespeare among them, having the status of "sharers" and the right to a share in the takings, as well as the responsibility for a part of the expenses. Five of the sharers themselves, Shakespeare among them, owned the Globe. As actor, as sharer in an acting company and in ownership of theaters, and as playwright, Shakespeare was about as involved in the theatrical industry as one could imagine. Although Shakespeare and his fellows prospered, their status under the law was conditional upon the protection of powerful patrons. "Common players"—those who did not have patrons or masters—were classed in the language of the law with "vagabonds and sturdy beggars." So the actors had to secure for themselves the official rank of servants of patrons. Among the patrons under whose protection Shakespeare's company worked were the lord chamberlain and, after the accession of King James in 1603, the king himself.

We are now perhaps on the verge of learning a great deal more about the theaters in which Shakespeare and his contemporaries performed—or at least of opening up new questions about them. Already about 70 percent of the Rose has been excavated, as has about 10 percent of the second Globe, the one built in 1614. It is to be hoped that soon more will be available for study. These are exciting times for students of Shakespeare's stage.

The Publication of Shakespeare's Plays

Eighteen of Shakespeare's plays found their way into print during the playwright's lifetime, but there is nothing to suggest that he took any interest in their publication. These eighteen appeared separately in editions called quartos. Their pages were not much larger than the one you are now reading, and these little books were sold unbound for a few pence. The earliest of the quartos that still survive were printed in 1594, the year that both *Titus Andronicus* and a version of the play now called *2 King Henry VI* became available. While almost every one of these early quartos displays on its title page the name of the acting company that performed the play, only about half provide the name of the playwright, Shakespeare. The first quarto edition to bear the name Shakespeare on its title page is *Love's Labor's Lost* of 1598. A few of these quartos were popular with the book-buying public of Shakespeare's lifetime; for example, quarto *Richard II* went through five editions between 1597 and 1615. But most of the quartos were far from best-sellers; *Love's Labor's Lost* (1598), for instance, was not reprinted in quarto until 1631. After Shakespeare's death, two more of his plays appeared in quarto format: *Othello* in 1622 and *The Two Noble Kinsmen*, coauthored with John Fletcher, in 1634.

In 1623, seven years after Shakespeare's death, *Mr. William Shakespeares Comedies, Histories, & Tragedies* was published. This printing offered readers in a single book thirty-six of the thirty-eight plays now thought to have been written by Shakespeare, including eighteen that had never been printed before. And it offered them in a style that was then reserved for serious literature and scholarship. The plays were arranged in double columns on pages nearly a foot high. This large page size is called "folio," as opposed to the smaller "quarto," and the 1623 volume is usually called the Shakespeare First Folio. It is reputed to have sold for the lordly price of a pound. (One copy at the Folger Library is marked fifteen shillings—that is, three-quarters of a pound.)

In a preface to the First Folio entitled "To the great Variety of Readers," two of Shakespeare's former fellow actors in the King's Men, John Heminge and Henry Condell, wrote that they themselves had collected their dead companion's plays. They suggested that they had seen his own papers: "we have scarce received from him a blot in his papers." The title page of the Folio declared

The Publication of Shakespeare's Plays

that the plays within it had been printed "according to the True Original Copies." Comparing the Folio to the quartos, Heminge and Condell disparaged the quartos, advising their readers that "before you were abused with divers stolen and surreptitious copies, maimed, and deformed by the frauds and stealths of injurious impostors." Many Shakespeareans of the eighteenth and nineteenth centuries believed Heminge and Condell and regarded the Folio plays as superior to anything in the quartos.

Once we begin to examine the Folio plays in detail, it becomes less easy to take at face value the word of Heminge and Condell about the superiority of the Folio texts. For example, of the first nine plays in the Folio (one quarter of the entire collection), four were essentially reprinted from earlier quarto printings that Heminge and Condell had disparaged; and four have now been identified as printed from copies written in the hand of a professional scribe of the 1620s named Ralph Crane; the ninth, *The Comedy of Errors*, was apparently also printed from a manuscript, but one whose origin cannot be readily identified. Evidently then, eight of the first nine plays in the First Folio were not printed, in spite of what the Folio title page announces, "according to the True Original Copies," or Shakespeare's own papers, and the source of the ninth is unknown. Since today's editors have been forced to treat Heminge and Condell's pronouncements with skepticism, they must choose whether to base their own editions upon quartos or the Folio on grounds other than Heminge and Condell's story of where the quarto and Folio versions originated.

Editors have often fashioned their own narratives to explain what lies behind the quartos and Folio. They have said that Heminge and Condell meant to criticize only a few of the early quartos, the ones that offer much shorter and sometimes quite different, often garbled, versions of plays. Among the examples of these are the 1600 quarto of *Henry V* (the Folio offers a much fuller version) or the 1603 *Hamlet* quarto (in 1604 a different, much longer form of the play got into print as a quarto). Early in this century editors speculated that these questionable texts were produced when someone in the audience took notes from the plays' dialogue during performances and then employed "hack poets" to fill out the notes. The poor results were then sold to a publisher and presented in print as Shakespeare's plays. More recently this story has given way to another in which the shorter versions are said to be recreations from memory of Shakespeare's plays by actors who wanted to stage them in the provinces but lacked manuscript copies. Most of the quartos offer much better texts than these so-called bad quartos. Indeed, in most of the quartos we find texts that are at least equal to or better than what is printed in the Folio. Many of this century's Shakespeare enthusiasts have persuaded themselves that most of the quartos were set into type directly from Shakespeare's own papers, although there is nothing on which to base this conclusion except the desire for it to be true. Thus speculation continues about how the Shakespeare plays got to be printed. All that we have are the printed texts.

The book collector who was most successful in bringing together copies of the quartos and the First Folio was Henry Clay Folger, founder of the Folger Shakespeare Library in Washington, D.C. While it is estimated that there survive around the world only about 230 copies of the First Folio, Mr. Folger was able to acquire more than seventy-five copies, as well as a large number of fragments, for the library that bears his name. He also amassed a substantial number of quartos. For example, only fourteen copies of the First Quarto of *Love's Labor's*

Lost are known to exist, and three are at the Folger Shakespeare Library. As a consequence of Mr. Folger's labors, twentieth-century scholars visiting the Folger Library have been able to learn a great deal about sixteenth- and seventeenth-century printing and, particularly, about the printing of Shakespeare's plays. And Mr. Folger did not stop at the First Folio, but collected many copies of later editions of Shakespeare, beginning with the Second Folio (1632), the Third (1663–64), and the Fourth (1685). Each of these later folios was based on its immediate predecessor and was edited anonymously. The first editor of Shakespeare whose name we know was Nicholas Rowe, whose first edition came out in 1709. Mr. Folger collected this edition and many, many more by Rowe's successors.

An Introduction to This Text

Twelfth Night, or, What You Will was first printed in the 1623 collection of Shakespeare's plays now known as the First Folio. The present edition is based directly upon the First Folio version.* For the convenience of the reader, we have modernized the punctuation and the spelling of the Folio. Sometimes we go so far as to modernize certain old forms of words; for example, when *a* means "he," we change it to *he;* we change *mo* to *more,* and *ye* to *you.* But it is not our practice in editing any of the plays to modernize words that sound distinctly different from modern forms. For example, when the

---

*We have also consulted the computerized text of the First Folio provided by the Text Archive of the Oxford University Computing Centre, to which we are grateful.

early printed texts read *sith* or *apricocks* or *porpentine*, we have not modernized to *since, apricots, porcupine*. When the forms *an, and,* or *and if* appear instead of the modern form *if*, we have reduced *and* to *an* but have not changed any of these forms to their modern equivalent, *if*. We also modernize and, where necessary, correct passages in foreign languages, unless an error in the early printed text can be reasonably explained as a joke. Whenever we change the wording of the First Folio or add anything to its stage directions, we mark the change by enclosing it in superior half-brackets (⌐¬). We want our readers to be immediately aware when we have intervened. (Only when we correct an obvious typographical error in the First Folio does the change not get marked.) Whenever we change the First Folio's wording or its punctuation so that the meaning changes, we list the change in the textual notes at the back of the book, even if all we have done is fix an obvious error. We regularize a number of the proper names, as is the usual practice in editions of the play. For example, although the character Viola enters once under the name "Violenta" in the First Folio, in our edition she is always designated "Viola."

This edition differs from many earlier ones in its efforts to aid the reader in imagining the play as a performance rather than as a series of actual events. Thus stage directions are written with reference to the stage. For example, when, in 2.2, Viola refuses to take the ring offered to her by Malvolio, he throws it before her. If we were representing the play as pure fiction, our stage direction would read *"He throws the ring to the ground,"* but because we are representing the play as a stage action, our stage direction reads, instead, *"He throws down the ring."* Whenever it is reasonably certain, in our view, that a speech is accompanied by a particular action, we provide a stage direction describing the action. (Occasional exceptions to this rule occur when the action is so obvious that to add a stage direction would insult the reader.) Stage directions for the entrance of characters in mid-scene are, with rare exceptions, placed so that they immediately precede the characters' participation in the scene, even though these entrances may appear somewhat earlier in the early printed texts. Whenever we move a stage direction, we record this change in the textual notes. Latin stage directions (e.g., *Exeunt*) are translated into English (e.g., *They exit*).

We expand the often severely abbreviated forms of names used as speech headings in early printed texts into the full names of the characters. We also regularize the speakers' names in speech headings, using only a single designation for each character, even though the early printed texts sometimes use a variety of designations. Variations in the speech headings of the early printed texts are recorded in the textual notes.

In the present edition, as well, we mark with a dash any change of address within a speech, unless a stage direction intervenes. When the *-ed* ending of a word is to be pronounced, we mark it with an accent. Like editors for the last two centuries, we print metrically linked lines in the following way:

VIOLA
  I think not so, my lord.
ORSINO   Dear lad, believe it.

However, when there are a number of short verse-lines that can be linked in more than one way, we do not, with rare exceptions, indent any of them.

The Explanatory Notes

The notes that appear on the pages facing the text are designed to provide readers with the help that they may need to enjoy the play. Whenever the meaning of a word in the text is not readily accessible in a good contemporary dictionary, we offer the meaning in a note. Sometimes we provide a note even when the relevant meaning is to be found in the dictionary but when the word has acquired since Shakespeare's time other potentially confusing meanings. In our notes, we try to offer modern synonyms for Shakespeare's words. We also try to indicate to the reader the connection between the word in the play and the modern synonym. For example, Shakespeare sometimes uses the word *head* to mean "source," but, for modern readers, there may be no connection evident between these two words. We provide the connection by explaining Shakespeare's usage as follows: "**head:** fountainhead, source." On some occasions, a whole phrase or clause needs explanation. Then we rephrase in our own words the difficult passage, and add at the end synonyms for individual words in the passage. When scholars have been unable to determine the meaning of a word or phrase, we acknowledge the uncertainty.

TWELFTH NIGHT,
OR,
WHAT YOU WILL

Characters in the Play

VIOLA, a lady of Messaline shipwrecked on the coast of Illyria (later disguised as CESARIO)

OLIVIA, an Illyrian countess
MARIA, her waiting-gentlewoman
SIR TOBY BELCH, Olivia's kinsman
SIR ANDREW AGUECHEEK, Sir Toby's companion
MALVOLIO, steward in Olivia's household
FOOL, Olivia's jester, named Feste
FABIAN, a gentleman in Olivia's household

ORSINO, duke (or count) of Illyria
VALENTINE } gentlemen serving Orsino
CURIO

SEBASTIAN, Viola's brother
ANTONIO, friend to Sebastian

CAPTAIN
PRIEST
TWO OFFICERS

Lords, Sailors, Musicians, and other Attendants

TWELFTH NIGHT,
OR,
WHAT YOU WILL

ACT 1

1.1 At his court, Orsino, sick with love for the Lady Olivia, learns from his messenger that she is grieving for her dead brother and refuses to be seen for seven years.

---

0 SD. **Illyria:** an ancient country in southern Europe, on the Adriatic Sea

2–3. **that . . . appetite:** i.e., so that my passion, glutted

4. **fall:** cadence (i.e., a sequence of chords ending the **strain** of music)

9–14. **O spirit . . . minute:** Love is described here as so hungry that it can devour everything and destroy the value of even the most precious things. **quick and fresh:** keen and eager (to devour) **validity:** worth **pitch:** i.e., excellence (The pitch is the highest point in a falcon's flight.)

14–15. **fancy, high fantastical: Fancy** is both "love" and "imagination"; **high fantastical** carries the sense both of "highly imaginative, most able to create powerful images," and "extremely passionate." Orsino seems to be playing with the double meanings of these related words as he tries to describe the intensity of his lovesickness.

18. **hart:** stag (Orsino, in the following line, plays on the fact that *hart* sounds like *heart*.)

ACT 1

Scene 1
*Enter Orsino, Duke of Illyria, Curio, and other Lords,
⌜with Musicians playing.⌝*

ORSINO
If music be the food of love, play on.
Give me excess of it, that, surfeiting,
The appetite may sicken and so die.
That strain again! It had a dying fall.
O, it came o'er my ear like the sweet sound   5
That breathes upon a bank of violets,
Stealing and giving odor. Enough; no more.
'Tis not so sweet now as it was before.
O spirit of love, how quick and fresh art thou,
That, notwithstanding thy capacity   10
Receiveth as the sea, naught enters there,
Of what validity and pitch soe'er,
But falls into abatement and low price
Even in a minute. So full of shapes is fancy
That it alone is high fantastical.   15

CURIO
Will you go hunt, my lord?
ORSINO   What, Curio?
CURIO   The hart.
ORSINO
Why, so I do, the noblest that I have.
O, when mine eyes did see Olivia first,   20

21. **Methought:** it seemed to me; **purged ... pestilence:** i.e., purified the air of everything infectious

22–24. **That instant ... pursue me:** Orsino compares himself to the mythological figure Acteon, who, having seen the goddess Diana bathing, was turned into a **hart** and destroyed by his own hounds. (See page 44.) **fell:** fierce, deadly

26. **So please my lord:** a polite phrase addressed to one's superior; **might not be:** i.e., was not

28. **element itself:** i.e., the very sky; **seven years' heat:** i.e., until seven summers have passed

30. **cloistress:** a nun in a cloister

32. **eye-offending brine:** i.e., tears; **season:** preserve, keep fresh (**Brine** is salt water used for preserving food.)

33. **brother's ... love:** i.e., love for her dead brother

36. **but to a:** i.e., to a mere

37. **golden shaft:** In the mythology of romantic love, anyone struck by Cupid's arrow with the golden head falls desperately in love. (See page 100.)

38. **affections else:** other feelings or desires

40. **thrones:** The **liver** was considered the seat of the passions, the **brain** the seat of reason, and the **heart** the seat of feeling.

40–41. **and ... perfections:** i.e., and her sweet perfections filled

41. **one self king:** a single monarch

1.2 On the Adriatic seacoast, Viola, who has been saved from a shipwreck in which her brother may
(continued)

Methought she purged the air of pestilence.
That instant was I turned into a hart,
And my desires, like fell and cruel hounds,
E'er since pursue me.

Enter Valentine.

How now, what news from her? 25

VALENTINE
So please my lord, I might not be admitted,
But from her handmaid do return this answer:
The element itself, till seven years' heat,
Shall not behold her face at ample view,
But like a cloistress she will veilèd walk, 30
And water once a day her chamber round
With eye-offending brine—all this to season
A brother's dead love, which she would keep fresh
And lasting in her sad remembrance.

ORSINO
O, she that hath a heart of that fine frame 35
To pay this debt of love but to a brother,
How will she love when the rich golden shaft
Hath killed the flock of all affections else
That live in her; when liver, brain, and heart,
These sovereign thrones, are all supplied, and filled 40
Her sweet perfections with one self king!
Away before me to sweet beds of flowers!
Love thoughts lie rich when canopied with bowers.
They exit.

Scene 2
Enter Viola, a Captain, and Sailors.

VIOLA What country, friends, is this?
CAPTAIN This is Illyria, lady.
VIOLA
And what should I do in Illyria?

have drowned, hears about Orsino and Olivia. She wishes to join Olivia's household, but is told that Olivia will admit no one into her presence. Viola decides to disguise herself as a boy so that she can join Orsino's male retinue.

---

4. **Elysium:** in Greek mythology, where the blessed go after death
5. **Perchance:** perhaps, possibly
7. **perchance:** i.e., by chance, through good luck
12. **driving:** i.e., drifting
15. **lived:** i.e., floated
16. **Arion . . . back:** Arion, a Greek poet and musician, so charmed the dolphins with his music that one saved him from drowning. (See page 188.)
20–22. **Mine . . . him:** i.e., my escape makes me hope that my brother escaped too, and your speech encourages that hope
31. **late:** recently

My brother he is in Elysium.
Perchance he is not drowned.—What think you,
sailors?
CAPTAIN
It is perchance that you yourself were saved.
VIOLA
O, my poor brother! And so perchance may he be.
CAPTAIN
True, madam. And to comfort you with chance,
Assure yourself, after our ship did split,
When you and those poor number saved with you
Hung on our driving boat, I saw your brother,
Most provident in peril, bind himself
(Courage and hope both teaching him the practice)
To a strong mast that lived upon the sea,
Where, like ⌜Arion⌝ on the dolphin's back,
I saw him hold acquaintance with the waves
So long as I could see.
VIOLA, ⌜*giving him money*⌝ For saying so, there's gold.
Mine own escape unfoldeth to my hope,
Whereto thy speech serves for authority,
The like of him. Know'st thou this country?
CAPTAIN
Ay, madam, well, for I was bred and born
Not three hours' travel from this very place.
VIOLA Who governs here?
CAPTAIN
A noble duke, in nature as in name.
VIOLA What is his name?
CAPTAIN Orsino.
VIOLA
Orsino. I have heard my father name him.
He was a bachelor then.
CAPTAIN
And so is now, or was so very late;
For but a month ago I went from hence,

34. **the less:** i.e., those of lower rank
38. **some twelvemonth since:** i.e., about a year ago
44. **delivered:** revealed
45. **mellow:** ripe
46. **estate:** social rank, position
47. **compass:** achieve, accomplish
48. **suit:** petition, formal request
51–52. **though . . . pollution:** i.e., although natural beauty often hides inner corruption
53–54. **suits / With:** corresponds with, matches
54. **character:** i.e., personal appearance and behavior
56. **Conceal me:** i.e., conceal, keep secret
57. **become:** be suitable to
59. **eunuch:** a male soprano or castrato
62. **allow . . . worth:** i.e., commend me as worthy to be in
64. **wit:** plan
65. **mute:** a person unable to speak

And then 'twas fresh in murmur (as, you know,
What great ones do the less will prattle of)
That he did seek the love of fair Olivia.

VIOLA What's she?

CAPTAIN
A virtuous maid, the daughter of a count
That died some twelvemonth since, then leaving her
In the protection of his son, her brother,
Who shortly also died, for whose dear love,
They say, she hath abjured the sight
And company of men.

VIOLA   O, that I served that lady,
And might not be delivered to the world
Till I had made mine own occasion mellow,
What my estate is.

CAPTAIN   That were hard to compass
Because she will admit no kind of suit,
No, not the Duke's.

VIOLA
There is a fair behavior in thee, captain,
And though that nature with a beauteous wall
Doth oft close in pollution, yet of thee
I will believe thou hast a mind that suits
With this thy fair and outward character.
I prithee—and I'll pay thee bounteously—
Conceal me what I am, and be my aid
For such disguise as haply shall become
The form of my intent. I'll serve this duke.
Thou shalt present me as an eunuch to him.
It may be worth thy pains, for I can sing
And speak to him in many sorts of music
That will allow me very worth his service.
What else may hap, to time I will commit.
Only shape thou thy silence to my wit.

CAPTAIN
Be you his eunuch, and your mute I'll be.

1.3 At the estate of Lady Olivia, Sir Toby Belch, Olivia's kinsman, has brought in Sir Andrew Aguecheek to be her suitor. Maria, Olivia's lady-in-waiting, says that Andrew is a fool, and Andrew himself doubts his ability to win Olivia, but Toby encourages him to woo her.

1, 5. **niece, cousin:** Both of these terms indicate close kinship; neither was as specific as it is today.

2. **care:** sorrow

4. **By my troth:** a mild oath

7. **except before excepted:** Toby's adaptation of the legal phrase *exceptis excipiendis* ("excepting those things which are to be excepted"), which he uses to dismiss Olivia's criticism

9. **modest:** moderate

10. **confine myself:** i.e., dress myself

12. **An:** if

14. **undo you:** ruin you; cause your downfall

20. **tall:** brave (Maria takes the word in its usual sense.)

22. **has . . . ducats:** i.e., has an income of three thousand gold coins

23. **have . . . ducats:** i.e., spend all his inheritance in a single year

24. **prodigal:** wastrel, spendthrift

25–26. **viol-de-gamboys:** i.e., viola da gamba, the predecessor of the modern cello (See page 60.)

27. **without book:** i.e., from memory

When my tongue blabs, then let mine eyes not see.
VIOLA I thank thee. Lead me on.

They exit.

Scene 3
Enter Sir Toby and Maria.

TOBY What a plague means my niece to take the death of her brother thus? I am sure care's an enemy to life.

MARIA By my troth, Sir Toby, you must come in earlier o' nights. Your cousin, my lady, takes great exceptions to your ill hours.

TOBY Why, let her except before excepted!

MARIA Ay, but you must confine yourself within the modest limits of order.

TOBY Confine? I'll confine myself no finer than I am. These clothes are good enough to drink in, and so be these boots too. An they be not, let them hang themselves in their own straps!

MARIA That quaffing and drinking will undo you. I heard my lady talk of it yesterday, and of a foolish knight that you brought in one night here to be her wooer.

TOBY Who, Sir Andrew Aguecheek?

MARIA Ay, he.

TOBY He's as tall a man as any 's in Illyria.

MARIA What's that to th' purpose?

TOBY Why, he has three thousand ducats a year!

MARIA Ay, but he'll have but a year in all these ducats. He's a very fool and a prodigal.

TOBY Fie, that you'll say so! He plays o' th' viol-de-gamboys, and speaks three or four languages word for word without book, and hath all the good gifts of nature.

29. **natural:** i.e., like a "natural" or idiot
30. **but that:** except for the fact that
31–32. **gust . . . in:** i.e., taste . . . for
34–35. **substractors:** i.e., detractors, slanderers
40. **coistrel:** lowborn contemptible fellow
42. **parish top:** a large public whipping-top (See page 186.); **Castiliano vulgo:** The meaning of this Spanish-sounding phrase (if it had one) is lost.
43. **Agueface:** This misnaming of Sir Andrew calls attention to the meaning of "Aguecheek," i.e., the pale, thin cheek (or face) of someone suffering from a fever or ague.
46. **shrew:** Andrew may be alluding to Maria's size (the shrew is among the smallest of mammals), or he may be using **shrew** (a word applied to a scolding or brawling woman) to mean simply "woman."
48. **Accost:** i.e., approach her, **woo her** (line 56) (In nautical terms, one ship accosts another by going alongside. The nautical language continues in **front** —i.e., confront—and **board** [line 55] and perhaps in **undertake** [line 57].)
60. **An . . . so:** i.e., if you let her leave so unceremoniously

MARIA He hath indeed, almost natural, for, besides that he's a fool, he's a great quarreler, and, but that he hath the gift of a coward to allay the gust he hath in quarreling, 'tis thought among the prudent he would quickly have the gift of a grave.

TOBY By this hand, they are scoundrels and substractors that say so of him. Who are they?

MARIA They that add, moreover, he's drunk nightly in your company.

TOBY With drinking healths to my niece. I'll drink to her as long as there is a passage in my throat and drink in Illyria. He's a coward and a coistrel that will not drink to my niece till his brains turn o' th' toe like a parish top. What, wench! *Castiliano vulgo*, for here comes Sir Andrew Agueface.

Enter Sir Andrew.

ANDREW Sir Toby Belch! How now, Sir Toby Belch?
TOBY Sweet Sir Andrew!
ANDREW, ⌜*to Maria*⌝ Bless you, fair shrew.
MARIA And you too, sir.
TOBY Accost, Sir Andrew, accost!
ANDREW What's that?
TOBY My niece's chambermaid.
⌜**ANDREW**⌝ Good Mistress Accost, I desire better acquaintance.
MARIA My name is Mary, sir.
ANDREW Good Mistress Mary Accost—
TOBY You mistake, knight. "Accost" is front her, board her, woo her, assail her.
ANDREW By my troth, I would not undertake her in this company. Is that the meaning of "accost"?
MARIA Fare you well, gentlemen. ⌜*She begins to exit.*⌝
TOBY An thou let part so, Sir Andrew, would thou mightst never draw sword again.
ANDREW An you part so, mistress, I would I might

64. **have fools in hand:** i.e., are dealing with fools

66. **Marry:** a mild oath, meaning "truly" or "indeed" (originally, an oath "by the Virgin Mary")

68. **thought is free:** a proverbial response to the question "Do you think I'm a fool?"

69. **butt'ry bar:** the ledge on top of the half door to the buttery, the storeroom for food and drink

71. **Wherefore:** i.e., why

73. **dry:** withered (indicating Andrew's lack of vigor, with a probable pun on **dry** as "thirsty")

76. **dry jest:** sarcastic or ironic joke

79. **barren:** i.e., no longer full of jests

80. **canary:** sweet wine

81. **put down:** snubbed, silenced

83. **put me down:** i.e., lay me out

84. **Christian:** often used, as here, to mean an ordinary human being

90. **Pourquoi:** French for "why"

92. **tongues:** i.e., foreign languages

93. **bearbaiting:** a blood sport in which dogs attack a bear chained to a stake (See page 98.)

18

never draw sword again. Fair lady, do you think you have fools in hand?
MARIA Sir, I have not you by th' hand.
ANDREW Marry, but you shall have, and here's my hand. ⌜*He offers his hand.*⌝
MARIA, ⌜*taking his hand*⌝ Now, sir, thought is free. I pray you, bring your hand to th' butt'ry bar and let it drink.
ANDREW Wherefore, sweetheart? What's your metaphor?
MARIA It's dry, sir.
ANDREW Why, I think so. I am not such an ass but I can keep my hand dry. But what's your jest?
MARIA A dry jest, sir.
ANDREW Are you full of them?
MARIA Ay, sir, I have them at my fingers' ends. Marry, now I let go your hand, I am barren. *Maria exits.*
TOBY O knight, thou lack'st a cup of canary! When did I see thee so put down?
ANDREW Never in your life, I think, unless you see canary put me down. Methinks sometimes I have no more wit than a Christian or an ordinary man has. But I am a great eater of beef, and I believe that does harm to my wit.
TOBY No question.
ANDREW An I thought that, I'd forswear it. I'll ride home tomorrow, Sir Toby.
TOBY *Pourquoi*, my dear knight?
ANDREW What is *"pourquoi"*? Do, or not do? I would I had bestowed that time in the tongues that I have in fencing, dancing, and bearbaiting. O, had I but followed the arts!
TOBY Then hadst thou had an excellent head of hair.
ANDREW Why, would that have mended my hair?
TOBY Past question, for thou seest it will not ⌜curl by⌝ nature.

100. **distaff:** staff used in spinning thread from wool or flax (See page 166.)

101. **huswife:** housewife (**Huswife,** pronounced "hussif," also had the sense of "hussy.")

103. **Faith:** a mild oath

105. **she'll ... me:** i.e., she does not want me; **Count:** i.e., Orsino, referred to as a duke in the first two scenes, but referred to hereafter in the dialogue as a count; **hard by:** nearby

108. **degree:** position; **estate:** fortune

111–12. **masques and revels:** entertainments, plays, dances

113. **kickshawses:** kickshaws, trifles (French: *quelques choses*)

117. **galliard:** a popular dance (See page 156.)

118. **caper:** leap (A **caper** is also a condiment used in sauces. Toby plays on this sense when he mentions **mutton.**)

120. **back-trick:** probably, a backward leap or caper

123. **like:** i.e., likely

124. **take ... picture:** i.e., get dusty, and therefore need a curtain to protect them (It is unclear who "Mistress Mall" might be.)

126–27. **coranto, jig, sink-a-pace:** names for various dances

128. **virtues:** accomplishments

130. **star of a galliard:** a dancing star; or, a star propitious for dancing

132. **dun-colored stock:** i.e., brown stocking

20

ANDREW But it becomes ⌜me⌝ well enough, does 't not?
TOBY Excellent! It hangs like flax on a distaff, and I hope to see a huswife take thee between her legs and spin it off.
ANDREW Faith, I'll home tomorrow, Sir Toby. Your niece will not be seen, or if she be, it's four to one she'll none of me. The Count himself here hard by woos her.
TOBY She'll none o' th' Count. She'll not match above her degree, neither in estate, years, nor wit. I have heard her swear 't. Tut, there's life in 't, man.
ANDREW I'll stay a month longer. I am a fellow o' th' strangest mind i' th' world. I delight in masques and revels sometimes altogether.
TOBY Art thou good at these kickshawses, knight?
ANDREW As any man in Illyria, whatsoever he be, under the degree of my betters, and yet I will not compare with an old man.
TOBY What is thy excellence in a galliard, knight?
ANDREW Faith, I can cut a caper.
TOBY And I can cut the mutton to 't.
ANDREW And I think I have the back-trick simply as strong as any man in Illyria.
TOBY Wherefore are these things hid? Wherefore have these gifts a curtain before 'em? Are they like to take dust, like Mistress Mall's picture? Why dost thou not go to church in a galliard and come home in a coranto? My very walk should be a jig. I would not so much as make water but in a sink-a-pace. What dost thou mean? Is it a world to hide virtues in? I did think, by the excellent constitution of thy leg, it was formed under the star of a galliard.
ANDREW Ay, 'tis strong, and it does indifferent well in a ⌜dun-colored⌝ stock. Shall we ⌜set⌝ about some revels?

135. **Taurus:** one of the twelve signs of the zodiac, which, at least according to Chaucer, governed the neck and the throat (See pages 64 and 136.)

1.4 At Orsino's court, Viola, disguised as a page and calling herself Cesario, has gained the trust of Orsino, who decides to send her to woo Olivia for him. Viola confides to the audience that she loves Orsino herself.

---

2. **Cesario:** the name chosen by Viola for her male disguise, which she will wear for the rest of the play; **be much advanced:** i.e., achieve advancement, promotion

5. **either . . . negligence:** i.e., are concerned either that he is whimsical or that I cannot serve him well **fear:** distrust, suspect **humor:** disposition, whim

12. **On your attendance:** i.e., at your service

13. **aloof:** i.e., aside, apart

14. **no less but all:** i.e., everything

16. **address . . . unto:** i.e., go to

18. **them:** i.e., Olivia's servants

19. **have audience:** i.e., are admitted to speak with her

TOBY What shall we do else? Were we not born under
  Taurus?
ANDREW Taurus? ⌜That's⌝ sides and heart.
TOBY No, sir, it is legs and thighs. Let me see thee
  caper. ⌜*Sir Andrew dances.*⌝ Ha, higher! Ha, ha,
  excellent!

They exit.

Scene 4
Enter Valentine, and Viola in man's attire ⌜as Cesario.⌝

VALENTINE If the Duke continue these favors towards
  you, Cesario, you are like to be much advanced. He
  hath known you but three days, and already you
  are no stranger.
VIOLA You either fear his humor or my negligence, that
  you call in question the continuance of his love. Is
  he inconstant, sir, in his favors?
VALENTINE No, believe me.
VIOLA I thank you.

Enter ⌜Orsino,⌝ Curio, and Attendants.

  Here comes the Count.
ORSINO Who saw Cesario, ho?
VIOLA On your attendance, my lord, here.
ORSINO, ⌜*to Curio and Attendants*⌝
  Stand you awhile aloof.—Cesario,
  Thou know'st no less but all. I have unclasped
  To thee the book even of my secret soul.
  Therefore, good youth, address thy gait unto her.
  Be not denied access. Stand at her doors
  And tell them, there thy fixèd foot shall grow
  Till thou have audience.
VIOLA   Sure, my noble lord,
  If she be so abandoned to her sorrow
  As it is spoke, she never will admit me.

23. **leap . . . bounds:** i.e., go beyond the limits of courtesy

24. **unprofited:** i.e., unsuccessful

26. **unfold:** reveal, disclose

27. **Surprise:** overcome, capture (a military term)

28. **become thee well:** be appropriate for you

29. **attend:** pay attention to

30. **nuncio's:** messenger's; **more grave aspect:** i.e., older or more serious face

34. **Diana:** the virgin goddess, here the personification of youth and beauty (See page 34.)

35. **rubious:** ruby red; **pipe:** i.e., voice

36. **organ:** i.e., voice (literally, vocal chords, larynx); **sound:** i.e., not cracked

37. **is semblative . . . part:** i.e., is like a woman (**Part** may be a theatrical term. In Shakespeare's theater, boys played women's parts.)

38. **thy constellation:** i.e., the stars that govern your success (or, that have shaped you)

39. **attend:** i.e., go along with

45. **barful strife:** i.e., an undertaking full of obstacles or "bars" (barriers)

1.5 Viola, in her disguise as Cesario, appears at Olivia's estate. Olivia allows Cesario to speak with her privately about Orsino's love. As Cesario presents Orsino's love-suit, Olivia falls in love with Cesario. She sends her steward, Malvolio, after Cesario with a ring.

---

0 SD. **Feste, the Fool:** In the Folio, this character,
(continued)

24

ORSINO
  Be clamorous and leap all civil bounds
  Rather than make unprofited return.
VIOLA
  Say I do speak with her, my lord, what then?   25
ORSINO
  O, then unfold the passion of my love.
  Surprise her with discourse of my dear faith.
  It shall become thee well to act my woes.
  She will attend it better in thy youth
  Than in a nuncio's of more grave aspect.   30
VIOLA
  I think not so, my lord.
ORSINO   Dear lad, believe it;
  For they shall yet belie thy happy years
  That say thou art a man. Diana's lip
  Is not more smooth and rubious, thy small pipe   35
  Is as the maiden's organ, shrill and sound,
  And all is semblative a woman's part.
  I know thy constellation is right apt
  For this affair.—Some four or five attend him,
  All, if you will, for I myself am best   40
  When least in company.—Prosper well in this
  And thou shalt live as freely as thy lord,
  To call his fortunes thine.
VIOLA   I'll do my best
  To woo your lady. ⌜*Aside.*⌝ Yet a barful strife!   45
  Whoe'er I woo, myself would be his wife.
                                        They exit.

Scene 5
Enter Maria and ⌜Feste, the Fool.⌝

MARIA Nay, either tell me where thou hast been, or I
  will not open my lips so wide as a bristle may enter

in stage directions and speech prefixes, is simply called "Clown" (an indication that the role was played by the troupe's comic actor). In dialogue, he is always called "Fool." He is at one point (in 2.4) referred to as "Feste, the jester," which leads some editors to name him "Feste" in speech prefixes and stage directions.

3. **in . . . excuse:** i.e., to defend you

6. **fear no colors:** proverbial for "fear nothing"

7. **Make . . . good:** i.e., prove that; explain that

9. **Lenten:** i.e., weak, poor (good enough only for Lent, a time of fasting)

12. **In the wars:** Military flags were called **colors.**

13. **foolery:** Feste is a professional fool; i.e., he makes his living by entertaining his aristocratic patron and by amusing others in the household, who reward him for his **foolery.** Feste's foolery depends primarily on the way he uses words.

17. **turned away:** i.e., dismissed

20. **for:** i.e., as for; **let . . . out:** i.e., may the warm weather of summer make it bearable

23. **if one break:** Maria plays on **points** as meaning the laces that hold up a man's breeches.

24. **gaskins:** breeches or hose

27. **piece of Eve's flesh:** i.e., woman

29. **you were best:** We would say: "If you know what's good for you."

30. **Wit:** i.e., intelligence, brain; **an 't:** i.e., if it

31. **wits:** clever people

33. **Quinapalus:** a philosopher invented by Feste

34. **witty:** clever

in way of thy excuse. My lady will hang thee for thy absence.

FOOL Let her hang me. He that is well hanged in this world needs to fear no colors.

MARIA Make that good.

FOOL He shall see none to fear.

MARIA A good Lenten answer. I can tell thee where that saying was born, of "I fear no colors."

FOOL Where, good Mistress Mary?

MARIA In the wars; and that may you be bold to say in your foolery.

FOOL Well, God give them wisdom that have it, and those that are Fools, let them use their talents.

MARIA Yet you will be hanged for being so long absent. Or to be turned away, is not that as good as a hanging to you?

FOOL Many a good hanging prevents a bad marriage, and, for turning away, let summer bear it out.

MARIA You are resolute, then?

FOOL Not so, neither, but I am resolved on two points.

MARIA That if one break, the other will hold, or, if both break, your gaskins fall.

FOOL Apt, in good faith, very apt. Well, go thy way. If Sir Toby would leave drinking, thou wert as witty a piece of Eve's flesh as any in Illyria.

MARIA Peace, you rogue. No more o' that. Here comes my lady. Make your excuse wisely, you were best.
⌈*She exits.*⌉

Enter Lady Olivia with Malvolio ⌈and Attendants.⌉

FOOL ⌈*aside*⌉ Wit, an 't be thy will, put me into good fooling! Those wits that think they have thee do very oft prove fools, and I that am sure I lack thee may pass for a wise man. For what says Quinapalus? "Better a witty Fool than a foolish wit."—God bless thee, lady!

38. **Go to:** an expression of impatience; **dry:** i.e., dull, not amusing

39. **dishonest:** dishonorable (i.e., unreliable)

40. **madonna:** my lady, madam (an Italian form of address)

42. **dry:** thirsty; **mend:** (1) reform; (2) repair

44. **botcher:** a tailor who repairs clothing

45. **is but:** is merely

49. **cuckold:** a man whose wife is unfaithful; **calamity:** i.e., one whom Fortune has deserted

50. **bade:** commanded (**Bade** is the past tense of "bid.")

53. **Misprision:** a mistake, an error

53–54. **cucullus . . . monachum:** Proverbial: "A cowl does not make a monk."

55. **motley:** multicolored garments worn by professional fools

58. **Dexteriously:** i.e., dexterously, easily

60. **catechize:** question rigorously

60–61. **Good . . . virtue:** i.e., my good, virtuous mouse (as if addressed to a young girl being catechized by the priest)

62. **want . . . idleness:** lack of other pastime; **bide:** abide, listen to

72. **mend:** improve

28

OLIVIA Take the Fool away.

FOOL Do you not hear, fellows? Take away the Lady.

OLIVIA Go to, you're a dry Fool. I'll no more of you. Besides, you grow dishonest.

FOOL Two faults, madonna, that drink and good counsel will amend. For give the dry Fool drink, then is the Fool not dry. Bid the dishonest man mend himself; if he mend, he is no longer dishonest; if he cannot, let the botcher mend him. Anything that's mended is but patched; virtue that transgresses is but patched with sin, and sin that amends is but patched with virtue. If that this simple syllogism will serve, so; if it will not, what remedy? As there is no true cuckold but calamity, so beauty's a flower. The Lady bade take away the Fool. Therefore, I say again, take her away.

OLIVIA Sir, I bade them take away you.

FOOL Misprision in the highest degree! Lady, *cucullus non facit monachum*. That's as much to say as, I wear not motley in my brain. Good madonna, give me leave to prove you a fool.

OLIVIA Can you do it?

FOOL Dexteriously, good madonna.

OLIVIA Make your proof.

FOOL I must catechize you for it, madonna. Good my mouse of virtue, answer me.

OLIVIA Well, sir, for want of other idleness, I'll bide your proof.

FOOL Good madonna, why mourn'st thou?

OLIVIA Good Fool, for my brother's death.

FOOL I think his soul is in hell, madonna.

OLIVIA I know his soul is in heaven, Fool.

FOOL The more fool, madonna, to mourn for your brother's soul, being in heaven. Take away the fool, gentlemen.

OLIVIA What think you of this Fool, Malvolio? Doth he not mend?

78. **no fox:** i.e., not clever

78–79. **pass . . . twopence:** i.e., bet tuppence

82–83. **put down . . . with:** i.e., defeated (in a battle of wits) by

83. **ordinary fool:** perhaps, a simpleton; or, perhaps, a Fool without an aristocratic patron

84. **out of his guard:** defenseless, without an answer (a fencing metaphor)

85–86. **minister . . . him:** give him opportunities

87. **crow:** cry out in pleasure; **set . . . Fools:** i.e., professional fools **set:** deliberate, intentional

88. **zanies:** (1) subordinate fools in comedies, whose function is to imitate the main comic character; (2) assistants, flatterers

90. **distempered:** diseased, disturbed; **generous:** high-minded

91. **free:** magnanimous

92. **bird-bolts:** blunt arrows

93. **allowed Fool:** i.e., a Fool who has been given permission always to speak freely

94–95. **known discreet man:** i.e., a man known to be judicious, wise

96. **Mercury . . . leasing:** i.e., may Mercury, god of trickery, endow you with the gift of lying

106. **madman:** i.e., nonsense

107. **suit:** love-plea

31   Twelfth Night   ACT 1. SC. 5

MALVOLIO Yes, and shall do till the pangs of death
shake him. Infirmity, that decays the wise, doth
ever make the better Fool.   75
FOOL God send you, sir, a speedy infirmity, for the
better increasing your folly! Sir Toby will be sworn
that I am no fox, but he will not pass his word for
twopence that you are no fool.
OLIVIA How say you to that, Malvolio?   80
MALVOLIO I marvel your Ladyship takes delight in
such a barren rascal. I saw him put down the other
day with an ordinary fool that has no more brain
than a stone. Look you now, he's out of his guard
already. Unless you laugh and minister occasion to   85
him, he is gagged. I protest I take these wise men
that crow so at these set kind of Fools no better than
the Fools' zanies.
OLIVIA O, you are sick of self-love, Malvolio, and taste
with a distempered appetite. To be generous, guilt-   90
less, and of free disposition is to take those things
for bird-bolts that you deem cannon bullets. There
is no slander in an allowed Fool, though he do
nothing but rail; nor no railing in a known discreet
man, though he do nothing but reprove.   95
FOOL Now Mercury endue thee with leasing, for thou
speak'st well of Fools!

Enter Maria.

MARIA Madam, there is at the gate a young gentleman
much desires to speak with you.
OLIVIA From the Count Orsino, is it?   100
MARIA I know not, madam. 'Tis a fair young man, and
well attended.
OLIVIA Who of my people hold him in delay?
MARIA Sir Toby, madam, your kinsman.
OLIVIA Fetch him off, I pray you. He speaks nothing   105
but madman. Fie on him! ⌜*Maria exits.*⌝ Go you,
Malvolio. If it be a suit from the Count, I am sick,

112. **Jove:** king of the Roman gods
114. **pia mater:** i.e., brain
115. **What:** i.e., who
119–20. **a plague . . . herring:** perhaps Toby's explanation for his having belched or hiccoughed
120. **sot:** fool
126. **an he will:** if he wants to
127. **it's all one:** i.e., it doesn't matter
130. **draught:** i.e., cup of wine; **above heat:** Wine was thought to warm the liver.
132. **crowner:** i.e., coroner; **sit o':** i.e., hold an inquest on

Jove. (1.5.112)
From Vincenzo Cartari, *Le vere e noue Imagini* . . . (1615).

or not at home; what you will, to dismiss it. (*Malvolio exits.*) Now you see, sir, how your fooling grows old, and people dislike it.

FOOL Thou hast spoke for us, madonna, as if thy eldest son should be a Fool, whose skull Jove cram with brains, for—here he comes—one of thy kin has a most weak *pia mater*.

Enter Sir Toby.

OLIVIA By mine honor, half drunk!—What is he at the gate, cousin?

TOBY A gentleman.

OLIVIA A gentleman? What gentleman?

TOBY 'Tis a gentleman here—a plague o' these pickle herring!—How now, sot?

FOOL Good Sir Toby.

OLIVIA Cousin, cousin, how have you come so early by this lethargy?

TOBY Lechery? I defy lechery. There's one at the gate.

OLIVIA Ay, marry, what is he?

TOBY Let him be the devil an he will, I care not. Give me faith, say I. Well, it's all one.   *He exits.*

OLIVIA What's a drunken man like, Fool?

FOOL Like a drowned man, a fool, and a madman. One draught above heat makes him a fool, the second mads him, and a third drowns him.

OLIVIA Go thou and seek the crowner and let him sit o' my coz, for he's in the third degree of drink: he's drowned. Go look after him.

FOOL He is but mad yet, madonna, and the Fool shall look to the madman.   ⌜*He exits.*⌝

Enter Malvolio.

MALVOLIO Madam, yond young fellow swears he will speak with you. I told him you were sick; he takes

147. **sheriff's post:** a large carved post
147–48. **the ... bench:** i.e., a bench-support
153. **will ... no:** i.e., whether you want to or not
154. **personage:** appearance
156. **squash:** unripe **peascod** (pea pod)
157. **codling:** unripe apple
158. **in standing ... man:** i.e., halfway between boy and man, like a tide between ebb and flow
159–60. **shrewishly:** This word usually means "like a bad-tempered woman," but here it seems to mean merely "like a woman."

Diana. (1.4.34)
From Robert Whitcombe, *Janua diuorum* (1678).

on him to understand so much, and therefore comes to speak with you. I told him you were asleep; he seems to have a foreknowledge of that too, and therefore comes to speak with you. What is to be said to him, lady? He's fortified against any denial.

OLIVIA Tell him he shall not speak with me.

MALVOLIO Has been told so, and he says he'll stand at your door like a sheriff's post and be the supporter to a bench, but he'll speak with you.

OLIVIA What kind o' man is he?

MALVOLIO Why, of mankind.

OLIVIA What manner of man?

MALVOLIO Of very ill manner. He'll speak with you, will you or no.

OLIVIA Of what personage and years is he?

MALVOLIO Not yet old enough for a man, nor young enough for a boy—as a squash is before 'tis a peascod, or a codling when 'tis almost an apple. 'Tis with him in standing water, between boy and man. He is very well-favored, and he speaks very shrewishly. One would think his mother's milk were scarce out of him.

OLIVIA
Let him approach. Call in my gentlewoman.

MALVOLIO Gentlewoman, my lady calls.   *He exits.*

Enter Maria.

OLIVIA
Give me my veil. Come, throw it o'er my face.
⌜*Olivia veils.*⌝
We'll once more hear Orsino's embassy.

Enter ⌜Viola.⌝

VIOLA The honorable lady of the house, which is she?

167. **Your will?:** i.e., what do you want?

172. **con:** memorize

173-74. **comptible . . . usage:** sensitive to even the smallest slight

178. **modest:** moderate

180. **comedian:** actor

182. **that I play:** i.e., that which I act

184. **usurp myself:** i.e., hold possession of myself wrongfully (Olivia's joking way of admitting that she is herself)

185-86. **usurp yourself:** i.e., wrongfully hold possession of yourself (in that you are refusing to marry and reproduce)

187. **reserve:** keep for yourself; **from:** i.e., not part of

190. **forgive you:** i.e., excuse you from reciting

194. **like:** i.e., likely

197. **be not mad:** This odd phrase may represent a scribal or printing error. Some editors omit the word **not**; others interpret "not" to mean "not entirely."

198. **'Tis . . . me:** i.e., I am not myself lunatic—under the influence of Luna, the moon (See page 134.)

199. **make one:** i.e., take part

201. **swabber:** a sailor who swabs the decks; **hull:** remain, like a ship with furled sails

OLIVIA Speak to me. I shall answer for her. Your will?

VIOLA Most radiant, exquisite, and unmatchable beauty—I pray you, tell me if this be the lady of the house, for I never saw her. I would be loath to cast away my speech, for, besides that it is excellently well penned, I have taken great pains to con it. Good beauties, let me sustain no scorn. I am very comptible, even to the least sinister usage.

OLIVIA Whence came you, sir?

VIOLA I can say little more than I have studied, and that question's out of my part. Good gentle one, give me modest assurance if you be the lady of the house, that I may proceed in my speech.

OLIVIA Are you a comedian?

VIOLA No, my profound heart. And yet, by the very fangs of malice, I swear I am not that I play. Are you the lady of the house?

OLIVIA If I do not usurp myself, I am.

VIOLA Most certain, if you are she, you do usurp yourself, for what is yours to bestow is not yours to reserve. But this is from my commission. I will on with my speech in your praise and then show you the heart of my message.

OLIVIA Come to what is important in 't. I forgive you the praise.

VIOLA Alas, I took great pains to study it, and 'tis poetical.

OLIVIA It is the more like to be feigned. I pray you, keep it in. I heard you were saucy at my gates, and allowed your approach rather to wonder at you than to hear you. If you be not mad, begone; if you have reason, be brief. 'Tis not that time of moon with me to make one in so skipping a dialogue.

MARIA Will you hoist sail, sir? Here lies your way.

VIOLA No, good swabber, I am to hull here a little

202. **giant:** perhaps a sarcastic reference to Maria's size

208. **office:** i.e., what you have been ordered to say

209. **alone . . . ear:** i.e., concerns no one but you

210. **taxation of:** i.e., demand that you pay; **olive:** olive branch, a symbol of peace and goodwill

212–13. **What would you?:** i.e., what do you want?

215. **my entertainment:** the way I was received

217. **divinity:** i.e., religious truth, theology; **profanation:** a violation of something sacred

220. **your text:** the scriptural passage on which you are to expound

222. **comfortable:** comforting

226. **by the method:** according to the division of the text in the table of contents

233–34. **such . . . present:** i.e., this is a portrait of me as I am at this moment

236. **in grain:** indelible (**Grain** was a "fast" or permanent dye.)

"I hold the olive in my hand." (1.5.210–11)
From Gilles Corrozet, *Hecatongraphie . . .* (1543).

longer.—Some mollification for your giant, sweet lady.

⌜OLIVIA⌝ Tell me your mind.

⌜VIOLA⌝ I am a messenger.

OLIVIA Sure you have some hideous matter to deliver when the courtesy of it is so fearful. Speak your office.

VIOLA It alone concerns your ear. I bring no overture of war, no taxation of homage. I hold the olive in my hand. My words are as full of peace as matter.

OLIVIA Yet you began rudely. What are you? What would you?

VIOLA The rudeness that hath appeared in me have I learned from my entertainment. What I am and what I would are as secret as maidenhead: to your ears, divinity; to any other's, profanation.

OLIVIA Give us the place alone. We will hear this divinity. ⌜*Maria and Attendants exit.*⌝ Now, sir, what is your text?

VIOLA Most sweet lady—

OLIVIA A comfortable doctrine, and much may be said of it. Where lies your text?

VIOLA In Orsino's bosom.

OLIVIA In his bosom? In what chapter of his bosom?

VIOLA To answer by the method, in the first of his heart.

OLIVIA O, I have read it; it is heresy. Have you no more to say?

VIOLA Good madam, let me see your face.

OLIVIA Have you any commission from your lord to negotiate with my face? You are now out of your text. But we will draw the curtain and show you the picture. ⌜*She removes her veil.*⌝ Look you, sir, such a one I was this present. Is 't not well done?

VIOLA Excellently done, if God did all.

OLIVIA 'Tis in grain, sir; 'twill endure wind and weather.

238. **blent:** blended

242. **leave . . . copy:** i.e., leave no children to carry on your beauty (Olivia responds as if **copy** here meant a written record.)

244. **divers schedules:** various lists

245. **utensil:** i.e., part of my body; **labeled:** described on paper and attached as a codicil

246. **item:** Latin for "likewise" (used to introduce each article in a formal inventory)

248. **praise:** perhaps, appraise

251. **if:** i.e., even if; **the devil:** perhaps a reference to Lucifer, the archangel who, through pride, led the revolt of the angels against God, and who, after his fall, was named Satan (Proverbial: "As proud as Lucifer.")

253. **but recompensed:** i.e., no more than returned on equal terms

255. **The nonpareil of beauty:** i.e., a beauty without equal

257. **fertile:** abundant

261. **estate:** fortune, status

262. **voices:** public opinion; **divulged:** spoken of; **free:** noble

263. **in dimension . . . nature:** i.e., in his physical shape

264. **A gracious:** an attractive

VIOLA
'Tis beauty truly blent, whose red and white
Nature's own sweet and cunning hand laid on.
Lady, you are the cruel'st she alive 240
If you will lead these graces to the grave
And leave the world no copy.

OLIVIA O, sir, I will not be so hard-hearted! I will give out divers schedules of my beauty. It shall be inventoried and every particle and utensil labeled 245 to my will: as, *item*, two lips indifferent red; *item*, two gray eyes, with lids to them; *item*, one neck, one chin, and so forth. Were you sent hither to praise me?

VIOLA
I see you what you are. You are too proud. 250
But, if you were the devil, you are fair.
My lord and master loves you. O, such love
Could be but recompensed though you were crowned
The nonpareil of beauty. 255

OLIVIA   How does he love me?

VIOLA With adorations, fertile tears,
With groans that thunder love, with sighs of fire.

OLIVIA
Your lord does know my mind. I cannot love him.
Yet I suppose him virtuous, know him noble, 260
Of great estate, of fresh and stainless youth;
In voices well divulged, free, learned, and valiant,
And in dimension and the shape of nature
A gracious person. But yet I cannot love him.
He might have took his answer long ago. 265

VIOLA
If I did love you in my master's flame,
With such a suff'ring, such a deadly life,
In your denial I would find no sense.
I would not understand it.

271. **willow cabin:** a small shelter made of willow (The **willow** is the symbol of grief for unrequited love.)

272. **call . . . house:** i.e., call out to Olivia, outside of whose **house** the **cabin** is built

273. **cantons:** i.e., cantos, ballads; **contemnèd:** disdained, viewed with contempt

275. **Hallow:** shout

276. **babbling . . . air:** i.e., Echo (the nymph who, in Greek mythology, pined away for love until only her voice was left to "babble")

279. **But . . . me:** i.e., unless you took pity on me

282. **fortunes:** (current) situation; **state:** social standing; or, condition in life

289. **fee'd post:** hired messenger

291. **Love:** i.e., may the god of love (Cupid); **make . . . flint:** i.e., turn . . . into flint; **that . . . love:** i.e., the man you will one day love

298. **give . . . blazon:** i.e., proclaim your high rank five times over (A **blazon** is a coat of arms.); **Soft:** an exclamation meaning "wait a minute"

300. **man:** i.e., servant

OLIVIA Why, what would you? 270

VIOLA
Make me a willow cabin at your gate
And call upon my soul within the house,
Write loyal cantons of contemnèd love
And sing them loud even in the dead of night,
Hallow your name to the reverberate hills 275
And make the babbling gossip of the air
Cry out "Olivia!" O, you should not rest
Between the elements of air and earth
But you should pity me.

OLIVIA You might do much. 280
What is your parentage?

VIOLA
Above my fortunes, yet my state is well.
I am a gentleman.

OLIVIA Get you to your lord.
I cannot love him. Let him send no more— 285
Unless perchance you come to me again
To tell me how he takes it. Fare you well.
I thank you for your pains. Spend this for me.
⌜*She offers money.*⌝

VIOLA
I am no fee'd post, lady. Keep your purse.
My master, not myself, lacks recompense. 290
Love make his heart of flint that you shall love,
And let your fervor, like my master's, be
Placed in contempt. Farewell, fair cruelty. *She exits.*

OLIVIA "What is your parentage?"
"Above my fortunes, yet my state is well. 295
I am a gentleman." I'll be sworn thou art.
Thy tongue, thy face, thy limbs, actions, and spirit
Do give thee fivefold blazon. Not too fast! Soft, soft!
Unless the master were the man. How now? 300
Even so quickly may one catch the plague?

308. **County's man:** count's servant
309. **Would I:** i.e., whether I wanted it; **I'll . . . it:** i.e., I do not want it
310. **flatter with:** i.e., encourage
313. **Hie thee:** hurry
317. **owe:** own

Acteon. (1.1.24)
From Ovid, *Le metamorphosi* . . . (1538).

Methinks I feel this youth's perfections
With an invisible and subtle stealth
To creep in at mine eyes. Well, let it be.—
What ho, Malvolio!

Enter Malvolio.

MALVOLIO   Here, madam, at your service.
OLIVIA
Run after that same peevish messenger,
The County's man. He left this ring behind him,
Would I or not. Tell him I'll none of it.
⌜*She hands him a ring.*⌝
Desire him not to flatter with his lord,
Nor hold him up with hopes. I am not for him.
If that the youth will come this way tomorrow,
I'll give him reasons for 't. Hie thee, Malvolio.
MALVOLIO   Madam, I will. *He exits.*
OLIVIA
I do I know not what, and fear to find
Mine eye too great a flatterer for my mind.
Fate, show thy force. Ourselves we do not owe.
What is decreed must be, and be this so.
⌜*She exits.*⌝

TWELFTH NIGHT,
OR,
WHAT YOU WILL

ACT 2

2.1 A young gentleman named Sebastian, who has recently been saved from a shipwreck in which his sister has been lost, sets off for Orsino's court. Antonio, the sailor who saved him, follows him, even though Antonio risks his own life to do so.

---

1. **will you not:** i.e., do you not wish
3. **By your patience:** a polite phrase, "with your permission"
4. **malignancy:** evil influence (astrological term, carried also in the preceding phrase, "My stars shine darkly over me.")
5. **distemper:** disturb, damage
10. **sooth:** i.e., truly; **My ... voyage:** the journey I've set for myself
11. **mere extravagancy:** no more than wandering
12. **modesty:** reserve, lack of presumption
13. **what ... keep in:** i.e., what I wish to hide
13–14. **it ... manners:** i.e., courtesy compels me
14. **the rather:** all the more
19. **in an:** i.e., within the same
22. **breach of the sea:** i.e., the breaking waves

ACT 2

Scene 1
Enter Antonio and Sebastian.

ANTONIO Will you stay no longer? Nor will you not that I go with you?

SEBASTIAN By your patience, no. My stars shine darkly over me. The malignancy of my fate might perhaps distemper yours. Therefore I shall crave of you your leave that I may bear my evils alone. It were a bad recompense for your love to lay any of them on you.

ANTONIO Let me yet know of you whither you are bound.

SEBASTIAN No, sooth, sir. My determinate voyage is mere extravagancy. But I perceive in you so excellent a touch of modesty that you will not extort from me what I am willing to keep in. Therefore it charges me in manners the rather to express myself. You must know of me, then, Antonio, my name is Sebastian, which I called Roderigo. My father was that Sebastian of Messaline whom I know you have heard of. He left behind him myself and a sister, both born in an hour. If the heavens had been pleased, would we had so ended! But you, sir, altered that, for some hour before you took me from the breach of the sea was my sister drowned.

ANTONIO Alas the day!

   26–27. with . . . that: i.e., believe too much in this admiring judgment of my sister's beauty
   28. publish: proclaim
   28–29. that envy . . . fair: i.e., that even the envious must call beautiful
   32. entertainment: reception as my guest
   34. murder me for my love: i.e., destroy me (1) in exchange for my love, or (2) because I care so much about you
   37. recovered: rescued
   39–40. so near . . . mother: i.e., so close to behaving like a woman
   41. will . . . me: will weep, thus revealing my weakness
   45. Else: otherwise

2.2 Malvolio finds the disguised Viola and "returns" the ring. Viola, alone, realizes that Olivia has fallen in love with Cesario and understands that Orsino, Olivia, and Viola/Cesario are now in a love triangle that she is helpless to resolve.

---

   0 SD. at several doors: i.e., through separate stage entrances
   4. arrived . . . hither: i.e., just reached this place

SEBASTIAN A lady, sir, though it was said she much resembled me, was yet of many accounted beautiful. But though I could not with such estimable wonder overfar believe that, yet thus far I will boldly publish her: she bore a mind that envy could not but call fair. She is drowned already, sir, with salt water, though I seem to drown her remembrance again with more.

ANTONIO Pardon me, sir, your bad entertainment.

SEBASTIAN O good Antonio, forgive me your trouble.

ANTONIO If you will not murder me for my love, let me be your servant.

SEBASTIAN If you will not undo what you have done—that is, kill him whom you have recovered—desire it not. Fare you well at once. My bosom is full of kindness, and I am yet so near the manners of my mother that, upon the least occasion more, mine eyes will tell tales of me. I am bound to the Count Orsino's court. Farewell. *He exits.*

ANTONIO
The gentleness of all the gods go with thee!
I have many enemies in Orsino's court,
Else would I very shortly see thee there.
But come what may, I do adore thee so
That danger shall seem sport, and I will go.
He exits.

Scene 2
Enter Viola and Malvolio, at several doors.

MALVOLIO Were not you even now with the Countess Olivia?

VIOLA Even now, sir. On a moderate pace I have since arrived but hither.

MALVOLIO She returns this ring to you, sir. You might

8. **a ... assurance:** a certainty that offers him no hope

8–9. **will none of:** i.e., will not have

11. **this:** i.e., this message of rejection; **Receive it so:** i.e., take the ring with this understanding.

12. **She ... it:** This response seems to be a resourceful lie by Viola.

19. **made ... me:** i.e., looked me over carefully

20. **had lost:** i.e., had made her lose

22. **cunning:** craftiness

23. **Invites:** encourages, tempts

24. **None of:** i.e., she will not have (See above, lines 8–9.)

25. **the man:** i.e., the one she loves

28. **the pregnant enemy:** i.e., the devil, who uses such deceits as **disguise** in his wicked practices **pregnant:** resourceful

29. **the proper false:** those who are unfaithful but handsome

30. **In ... forms:** i.e., to imprint their images in women's impressionable hearts

31–32. **our ... be:** Proverbial: "Women are the weaker vessels."

33. **fadge:** i.e., work out, fit together

34. **monster:** i.e., a man/woman; **fond ... on:** just as infatuated with

37. **My ... for:** i.e., it is impossible that I should win

have saved me my pains to have taken it away
yourself. She adds, moreover, that you should put
your lord into a desperate assurance she will none
of him. And one thing more, that you be never so
hardy to come again in his affairs, unless it be to　10
report your lord's taking of this. Receive it so.
VIOLA She took the ring of me. I'll none of it.
MALVOLIO Come, sir, you peevishly threw it to her, and
her will is it should be so returned. ⌜*He throws
down the ring.*⌝ If it be worth stooping for, there it　15
lies, in your eye; if not, be it his that finds it.
He exits.

VIOLA
I left no ring with her. What means this lady?
　　　　　　　　⌜*She picks up the ring.*⌝
Fortune forbid my outside have not charmed her!
She made good view of me, indeed so much
That methought her eyes had lost her tongue,　20
For she did speak in starts distractedly.
She loves me, sure! The cunning of her passion
Invites me in this churlish messenger.
None of my lord's ring? Why, he sent her none!
I am the man. If it be so, as 'tis,　25
Poor lady, she were better love a dream.
Disguise, I see thou art a wickedness
Wherein the pregnant enemy does much.
How easy is it for the proper false
In women's waxen hearts to set their forms!　30
Alas, ⌜our⌝ frailty is the cause, not we,
For such as we are made ⌜of,⌝ such we be.
How will this fadge? My master loves her dearly,
And I, poor monster, fond as much on him,
And she, mistaken, seems to dote on me.　35
What will become of this? As I am man,
My state is desperate for my master's love.
As I am woman (now, alas the day!),

39. **thriftless:** useless, fruitless

2.3 At Olivia's estate, Toby, Andrew, and the Fool hold a late night party. Maria comes in to quiet them, followed by Malvolio, who orders them to behave or be dismissed from the house. In retaliation, Maria plots to trap Malvolio with a forged letter that will persuade him that Olivia loves him.

---

2. **betimes:** early
2-3. **diluculo surgere:** the first two words of a familiar Latin sentence that means "To rise early is good for the health"
6. **as:** i.e., as much as I do; **can:** drinking cup
9-10. **the . . . elements:** air, earth, water, and fire
14. **stoup:** tankard (a large drinking vessel)
17. **"We Three":** a familiar picture of two fools, the title of which, "We Three," suggests that the viewer is the third fool
18. **catch:** music written for three voices, sung as a round
19. **breast:** i.e., breath, singing voice
22. **fooling:** See note on **foolery** at 1.5.13.
23-24. **Pigrogromitus . . . Queubus:** examples of the Fool's wordplay (here, apparent mockery of astrological language)
25. **leman:** mistress, lover

54

What thriftless sighs shall poor Olivia breathe!
O Time, thou must untangle this, not I.
It is too hard a knot for me t' untie.

⌜*She exits.*⌝

Scene 3
Enter Sir Toby and Sir Andrew.

TOBY Approach, Sir Andrew. Not to be abed after midnight is to be up betimes, and *"diluculo surgere,"* thou know'st—

ANDREW Nay, by my troth, I know not. But I know to be up late is to be up late.

TOBY A false conclusion. I hate it as an unfilled can. To be up after midnight and to go to bed then, is early, so that to go to bed after midnight is to go to bed betimes. Does not our lives consist of the four elements?

ANDREW Faith, so they say, but I think it rather consists of eating and drinking.

TOBY Thou'rt a scholar. Let us therefore eat and drink. Marian, I say, a stoup of wine!

Enter ⌜*Feste, the Fool.*⌝

ANDREW Here comes the Fool, i' faith.

FOOL How now, my hearts? Did you never see the picture of "We Three"?

TOBY Welcome, ass! Now let's have a catch.

ANDREW By my troth, the Fool has an excellent breast. I had rather than forty shillings I had such a leg, and so sweet a breath to sing, as the Fool has.—In sooth, thou wast in very gracious fooling last night when thou spok'st of Pigrogromitus, of the Vapians passing the equinoctial of Queubus. 'Twas very good, i' faith. I sent thee sixpence for thy leman. Hadst it?

27. **impeticos thy gratillity:** more of the Fool's wordplay (**Gratillity** sounds like "gratuity," i.e., tip.)

27–29. **for . . . houses:** apparent nonsense to please Sir Andrew **whipstock:** whip handle **white:** then synonymous with "beautiful" **Myrmidons:** the followers of Achilles, the Greek warrior in Homer's *Iliad* **bottle-ale houses:** inferior taverns

34. **testril:** tester, sixpence; **of:** from

35. **give a:** In the Folio, there is no punctuation after these words, which come at the end of the line. It is possible that the next line of Andrew's speech was simply dropped.

36–37. **song . . . life:** a drinking song (Andrew, at line 39, appears to understand **good life** to mean a moral life.)

40. **"O mistress mine":** Tunes by this name were published in Shakespeare's time, but the words here are thought to be Shakespeare's.

44. **in lovers meeting:** i.e., when lovers meet

48. **hereafter:** at some future time

50. **still:** always

55. **contagious:** foul (but understood by Andrew to be a compliment)

57. **To . . . nose:** i.e., if we heard with our noses

58. **welkin:** heavens (See page 152.)

59. **catch:** See note to line 18, page 54.

60. **weaver:** Weavers were said to be fond of singing.

FOOL I did impeticos thy gratillity, for Malvolio's nose is no whipstock, my lady has a white hand, and the Myrmidons are no bottle-ale houses.
ANDREW Excellent! Why, this is the best fooling when all is done. Now, a song.
TOBY, ⌜*giving money to the Fool*⌝ Come on, there is sixpence for you. Let's have a song.
ANDREW, ⌜*giving money to the Fool*⌝ There's a testril of me, too. If one knight give a—
FOOL Would you have a love song or a song of good life?
TOBY A love song, a love song.
ANDREW Ay, ay, I care not for good life.
FOOL *sings*

    O mistress mine, where are you roaming?
    O, stay and hear! Your truelove's coming,
      That can sing both high and low.
    Trip no further, pretty sweeting.
    Journeys end in lovers meeting,
      Every wise man's son doth know.

ANDREW Excellent good, i' faith.
TOBY Good, good.
FOOL ⌜*sings*⌝

    What is love? 'Tis not hereafter.
    Present mirth hath present laughter.
      What's to come is still unsure.
    In delay there lies no plenty,
    Then come kiss me, sweet and twenty.
      Youth's a stuff will not endure.

ANDREW A mellifluous voice, as I am true knight.
TOBY A contagious breath.
ANDREW Very sweet and contagious, i' faith.
TOBY To hear by the nose, it is dulcet in contagion. But shall we make the welkin dance indeed? Shall we rouse the night owl in a catch that will draw three souls out of one weaver? Shall we do that?

61. **An:** if; **dog:** i.e., expert

63. **By 'r Lady:** an oath, "By our Lady" (i.e., the Virgin Mary)

64–65. **"Thou Knave":** a catch in which the singers call each other, in turn, "thou knave" (**Knave** meant variously "servant, menial," "boy," and "villain.")

76. **Cataian:** i.e., untrustworthy boaster (alluding to explorers who mistakenly claimed they had discovered riches in places they believed to be Cathay, or China); **politicians:** shrewd fellows

77. **Peg-a-Ramsey:** the name of a popular song

77–78. **Three . . . we:** a line from another popular song

78–79. **of her blood:** related to her (i.e., **consanguineous**)

79. **Tillyvally:** an expression of impatience; **"Lady":** Toby's mockery of Maria's reference to Olivia

79–80. **There . . . lady:** a line from a popular song

81. **Beshrew me:** i.e., curse me (a mild oath)

84. **natural:** i.e., naturally (with an unintended pun on "natural" meaning "like an idiot")

87. **My masters:** i.e., gentlemen

88. **wit:** sense; **honesty:** decency, decorum

89. **tinkers:** wandering menders of utensils, known for their drinking

91. **coziers:** cobblers

91–92. **mitigation or remorse:** These words suggest "softening," but neither seems appropriate as used here to refer to the **voice. Mitigation** is usually applied to a lessening of violence or disease; **re-**
(continued)

Twelfth Night — ACT 2. SC. 3

ANDREW An you love me, let's do 't. I am dog at a catch.

FOOL By 'r Lady, sir, and some dogs will catch well.

ANDREW Most certain. Let our catch be "Thou Knave."

FOOL "Hold thy peace, thou knave," knight? I shall be constrained in 't to call thee "knave," knight.

ANDREW 'Tis not the first time I have constrained one to call me "knave." Begin, Fool. It begins "Hold thy peace."

FOOL I shall never begin if I hold my peace.

ANDREW Good, i' faith. Come, begin.   *Catch sung.*

Enter Maria.

MARIA What a caterwauling do you keep here! If my lady have not called up her steward Malvolio and bid him turn you out of doors, never trust me.

TOBY My lady's a Cataian, we are politicians, Malvolio's a Peg-a-Ramsey, and ⌜*Sings.*⌝ *Three merry men be we.* Am not I consanguineous? Am I not of her blood? Tillyvally! "Lady"! ⌜*Sings.*⌝ *There dwelt a man in Babylon, lady, lady.*

FOOL Beshrew me, the knight's in admirable fooling.

ANDREW Ay, he does well enough if he be disposed, and so do I, too. He does it with a better grace, but I do it more natural.

TOBY ⌜*sings*⌝ *O' the twelfth day of December—*

MARIA For the love o' God, peace!

Enter Malvolio.

MALVOLIO My masters, are you mad? Or what are you? Have you no wit, manners, nor honesty but to gabble like tinkers at this time of night? Do you make an ale-house of my lady's house, that you squeak out your coziers' catches without any mitigation or remorse of voice? Is there no respect of place, persons, nor time in you?

morse is a theological term that applies to the conscience of a sinner. Malvolio's language often has odd quirks that contemporary audiences might have associated with his supposed puritanism. (See line 139.)

94. **Sneck up:** i.e., shut up

95. **round:** straightforward

102. **Farewell . . . gone:** the beginning of a song called "Corydon's Farewell to Phyllis," which continues through line 112.

107. **lie:** i.e., do not tell the truth (In "Corydon's Farewell," the words are "So long as I can spy.")

115. **cakes and ale:** associated with festivity

116. **Saint Anne:** mother of the Virgin Mary; **ginger:** used to spice ale

118–19. **rub . . . crumbs:** i.e., polish your steward's chain

A "viol-de-gamboys." (1.3.25–26)
From *Nieuwen ieucht spieghel . . .* (ca. 1620).

TOBY We did keep time, sir, in our catches. Sneck up!
MALVOLIO Sir Toby, I must be round with you. My lady bade me tell you that, though she harbors you as her kinsman, she's nothing allied to your disorders. If you can separate yourself and your misdemeanors, you are welcome to the house; if not, an it would please you to take leave of her, she is very willing to bid you farewell.
TOBY ⌈sings⌉
  Farewell, dear heart, since I must needs be gone.
MARIA Nay, good Sir Toby.
FOOL ⌈sings⌉
  His eyes do show his days are almost done.
MALVOLIO Is 't even so?
TOBY ⌈sings⌉
  But I will never die.
FOOL ⌈sings⌉
  Sir Toby, there you lie.
MALVOLIO This is much credit to you.
TOBY ⌈sings⌉
  Shall I bid him go?
FOOL ⌈sings⌉
  What an if you do?
TOBY ⌈sings⌉
  Shall I bid him go, and spare not?
FOOL ⌈sings⌉
  O no, no, no, no, you dare not.
TOBY Out o' tune, sir? You lie. Art any more than a steward? Dost thou think, because thou art virtuous, there shall be no more cakes and ale?
FOOL Yes, by Saint Anne, and ginger shall be hot i' th' mouth, too.
TOBY Thou'rt i' th' right.—Go, sir, rub your chain with crumbs.—A stoup of wine, Maria!
MALVOLIO Mistress Mary, if you prized my lady's favor at anything more than contempt, you would not give

122. **uncivil rule:** uncivilized conduct

125–28. **'Twere ... him:** In confused language (e.g., he means "thirsty" when he says **a-hungry**), Andrew threatens to challenge Malvolio to a duel and then not show up.

133. **out of quiet:** disquieted, troubled

133–34. **let ... him:** i.e., leave him to me

134. **gull ... nayword:** i.e., through trickery turn him into a byword (a figure of scorn)

135. **recreation:** i.e., figure of fun

138. **Possess:** inform

139. **puritan:** originally, a term of abuse used against members of the Church of England who were strict moralists, intent on stamping out sin and doing away with frivolity (The word comes from the Latin *purus*, "pure.")

145. **The devil ... is:** i.e., he is not a puritan

146. **constantly:** consistently; **time-pleaser:** flatterer, self-server; **affectioned:** affected

147. **cons ... book:** i.e., memorizes high-sounding phrases

148. **best ... of:** i.e., holding the highest opinion of

156. **expressure:** expression

means for this uncivil rule. She shall know of it, by
this hand. *He exits.*

MARIA Go shake your ears!

ANDREW 'Twere as good a deed as to drink when a
man's a-hungry, to challenge him the field and
then to break promise with him and make a fool of
him.

TOBY Do 't, knight. I'll write thee a challenge. Or I'll
deliver thy indignation to him by word of mouth.

MARIA Sweet Sir Toby, be patient for tonight. Since the
youth of the Count's was today with my lady, she is
much out of quiet. For Monsieur Malvolio, let me
alone with him. If I do not gull him into ⌜a nayword⌝
and make him a common recreation, do not think I
have wit enough to lie straight in my bed. I know I
can do it.

TOBY Possess us, possess us, tell us something of him.

MARIA Marry, sir, sometimes he is a kind of puritan.

ANDREW O, if I thought that, I'd beat him like a dog!

TOBY What, for being a puritan? Thy exquisite reason,
dear knight?

ANDREW I have no exquisite reason for 't, but I have
reason good enough.

MARIA The devil a puritan that he is, or anything
constantly but a time-pleaser; an affectioned ass
that cons state without book and utters it by great
swaths; the best persuaded of himself, so crammed,
as he thinks, with excellencies, that it is his grounds
of faith that all that look on him love him. And on
that vice in him will my revenge find notable cause
to work.

TOBY What wilt thou do?

MARIA I will drop in his way some obscure epistles of
love, wherein by the color of his beard, the shape of
his leg, the manner of his gait, the expressure of his
eye, forehead, and complexion, he shall find himself

158. **personated:** represented
159-60. **on . . . hands:** i.e., when we have forgotten who wrote something, we can barely distinguish her handwriting from mine
161. **device:** plan, scheme
170. **physic:** medicine
173. **construction:** interpretation
175. **Penthesilea:** queen of the Amazons (fierce warrior women)
176. **Before me:** a mild oath
182. **recover:** obtain
182-83. **a foul way out:** i.e., in financial trouble (literally, out in the dirt)
185. **Cut:** a horse (with a docked tail; or, gelded)
188. **burn some sack:** warm up some sherry

Taurus. (1.3.135)
From Johann Engel, *Astrolabium* (1488).

most feelingly personated. I can write very like my lady your niece; on a forgotten matter, we can hardly make distinction of our hands.

TOBY Excellent! I smell a device.

ANDREW I have 't in my nose, too.

TOBY He shall think, by the letters that thou wilt drop, that they come from my niece, and that she's in love with him.

MARIA My purpose is indeed a horse of that color.

ANDREW And your horse now would make him an ass.

MARIA Ass, I doubt not.

ANDREW O, 'twill be admirable!

MARIA Sport royal, I warrant you. I know my physic will work with him. I will plant you two, and let the Fool make a third, where he shall find the letter. Observe his construction of it. For this night, to bed, and dream on the event. Farewell.

TOBY Good night, Penthesilea. *She exits.*

ANDREW Before me, she's a good wench.

TOBY She's a beagle true bred, and one that adores me. What o' that?

ANDREW I was adored once, too.

TOBY Let's to bed, knight. Thou hadst need send for more money.

ANDREW If I cannot recover your niece, I am a foul way out.

TOBY Send for money, knight. If thou hast her not i' th' end, call me "Cut."

ANDREW If I do not, never trust me, take it how you will.

TOBY Come, come, I'll go burn some sack. 'Tis too late to go to bed now. Come, knight; come, knight.
They exit.

2.4 Orsino asks for a song to relieve his love-longing. In conversation about the capacities for love in men and in women, Viola expresses her love for Orsino through a story about "Cesario's sister." Orsino becomes curious about this sister's fate, but then turns back to his own longings and sends Cesario once again to visit Olivia.

1–2. **good morrow:** good morning

4. **antique:** old-fashioned (accent on first syllable)

5. **passion:** emotional suffering

6. **airs:** tunes, melodies; **recollected terms:** perhaps, unspontaneous or studied verse

20. **Unstaid and skittish:** fickle, inconstant; **in . . . else:** in all other emotions or desires

23. **It . . . echo:** i.e., it echoes exactly

23–24. **the seat . . . throned:** i.e., the lover's heart

27. **stayed . . . favor:** lingered over some face

29. **by your favor:** a courteous phrase, "if you please," with a punning reference to Orsino's "favor," or face

Scene 4

Enter ⌜Orsino,⌝ Viola, Curio, and others.

ORSINO
Give me some music. ⌜*Music plays.*⌝ Now, good
  morrow, friends.—
Now, good Cesario, but that piece of song,
That old and antique song we heard last night.
Methought it did relieve my passion much, 5
More than light airs and recollected terms
Of these most brisk and giddy-pacèd times.
Come, but one verse.

CURIO He is not here, so please your Lordship, that
  should sing it. 10

ORSINO Who was it?

CURIO Feste the jester, my lord, a Fool that the Lady
  Olivia's father took much delight in. He is about
  the house.

ORSINO
Seek him out ⌜*Curio exits,*⌝ and play the tune the 15
  while.   *Music plays.*
⌜*To Viola.*⌝ Come hither, boy. If ever thou shalt love,
In the sweet pangs of it remember me,
For such as I am, all true lovers are,
Unstaid and skittish in all motions else 20
Save in the constant image of the creature
That is beloved. How dost thou like this tune?

VIOLA
It gives a very echo to the seat
Where love is throned.

ORSINO   Thou dost speak masterly. 25
My life upon 't, young though thou art, thine eye
Hath stayed upon some favor that it loves.
Hath it not, boy?

VIOLA   A little, by your favor.

31. **complexion:** temperament; appearance
34. **still:** always
35. **wears . . . him:** i.e., shapes herself to fit him (like a garment to its owner)
36. **sways she level:** The image may be of a ruler holding sway, or of a balance scale.
38. **fancies:** loves
43. **hold the bent:** i.e., endure at its maximum tension, like a fully stretched bow (See page 70.)
45. **Being . . . displayed:** i.e., having blossomed
49. **Mark:** pay attention to
50. **spinsters:** those who spin thread or yarn
51. **free:** carefree
51–52. **weave . . . bones:** use bone bobbins in making lace
53. **Do use to:** customarily; **silly sooth:** simple truth
54. **dallies:** plays
55. **the old age:** i.e., the good old days

A balance scale. (2.4.36)
From Silvestro Pietrasanta, *Symbola heroica* (1682).

ORSINO
  What kind of woman is 't?
VIOLA   Of your complexion.
ORSINO
  She is not worth thee, then. What years, i' faith?
VIOLA   About your years, my lord.
ORSINO
  Too old, by heaven. Let still the woman take
  An elder than herself. So wears she to him;
  So sways she level in her husband's heart.
  For, boy, however we do praise ourselves,
  Our fancies are more giddy and unfirm,
  More longing, wavering, sooner lost and worn,
  Than women's are.
VIOLA   I think it well, my lord.
ORSINO
  Then let thy love be younger than thyself,
  Or thy affection cannot hold the bent.
  For women are as roses, whose fair flower,
  Being once displayed, doth fall that very hour.
VIOLA
  And so they are. Alas, that they are so,
  To die even when they to perfection grow!

Enter Curio and ⌜Feste, the Fool.⌝

ORSINO
  O, fellow, come, the song we had last night.—
  Mark it, Cesario. It is old and plain;
  The spinsters and the knitters in the sun
  And the free maids that weave their thread with
    bones
  Do use to chant it. It is silly sooth,
  And dallies with the innocence of love
  Like the old age.
FOOL   Are you ready, sir?
ORSINO   Ay, prithee, sing.   *Music.*

59. **sad cypress:** i.e., a coffin of dark cypress wood

62. **yew:** i.e., sprigs of yew (The yew tree was often planted in churchyards and was a symbol of sadness.)

67. **strown:** strewn

74. **There's for:** i.e., there's payment for

77–78. **pleasure . . . another:** i.e., pleasure must eventually be paid for (proverbial)

79. **Give . . . thee:** a polite request for the Fool to leave

80. **the . . . god:** i.e., Saturn, god of melancholy

81. **doublet:** jacket; **changeable taffeta:** a thin silky fabric woven so that the color appears to change when viewed from different perspectives

82. **opal:** a stone of variable colors

82–83. **such constancy:** i.e., so little constancy

84. **intent:** i.e., intended destination

A bow at the full bent. (2.4.43)
From Jacobus a. Bruck, *Emblemata moralia & bellica* (1615).

The Song.

⌜FOOL⌝
*Come away, come away, death,
 And in sad cypress let me be laid.
⌜Fly⌝ away, ⌜fly⌝ away, breath,
 I am slain by a fair cruel maid.
My shroud of white, stuck all with yew,
 O, prepare it!
My part of death, no one so true
 Did share it.*

*Not a flower, not a flower sweet
 On my black coffin let there be strown;
Not a friend, not a friend greet
 My poor corpse, where my bones shall be thrown.
A thousand thousand sighs to save,
 Lay me, O, where
Sad true lover never find my grave,
 To weep there.*

ORSINO, ⌜*giving money*⌝ There's for thy pains.
FOOL No pains, sir. I take pleasure in singing, sir.
ORSINO I'll pay thy pleasure, then.
FOOL Truly, sir, and pleasure will be paid, one time or another.
ORSINO Give me now leave to leave thee.
FOOL Now the melancholy god protect thee, and the tailor make thy doublet of changeable taffeta, for thy mind is a very opal. I would have men of such constancy put to sea, that their business might be everything and their intent everywhere, for that's it that always makes a good voyage of nothing. Farewell. *He exits.*
ORSINO
Let all the rest give place.
⌜*All but Orsino and Viola exit.*⌝
Once more, Cesario,

89. **sovereign cruelty:** (1) the cruel woman who rules my life; (2) the queen of cruelty (Orsino speaks the exaggerated language of love poetry.)
91. **quantity ... lands:** i.e., her property
92. **parts ... her:** i.e., her wealth and status
93. **hold as giddily as fortune:** Fortune is proverbially fickle. (See page 142.)
94–95. **that miracle ... in:** i.e., her own beauty, a gift of nature   **pranks:** dresses
102. **be answered:** i.e., take that as final
104. **bide:** endure
108. **No ... palate:** i.e., not a strong emotion whose seat is in the liver, but a casual appetite
109. **suffer:** experience; **revolt:** revulsion
111–12. **Make ... Between:** i.e., do not compare
113. **that:** i.e., that which
117. **In faith:** a mild oath

Get thee to yond same sovereign cruelty.
Tell her my love, more noble than the world, 90
Prizes not quantity of dirty lands.
The parts that fortune hath bestowed upon her,
Tell her, I hold as giddily as fortune.
But 'tis that miracle and queen of gems
That nature pranks her in attracts my soul. 95

VIOLA But if she cannot love you, sir—
ORSINO ⌈I⌉ cannot be so answered.
VIOLA   Sooth, but you must.
Say that some lady, as perhaps there is,
Hath for your love as great a pang of heart 100
As you have for Olivia. You cannot love her;
You tell her so. Must she not then be answered?
ORSINO There is no woman's sides
Can bide the beating of so strong a passion
As love doth give my heart; no woman's heart 105
So big, to hold so much; they lack retention.
Alas, their love may be called appetite,
No motion of the liver, but the palate,
That suffer surfeit, cloyment, and revolt;
But mine is all as hungry as the sea, 110
And can digest as much. Make no compare
Between that love a woman can bear me
And that I owe Olivia.
VIOLA   Ay, but I know—
ORSINO What dost thou know? 115
VIOLA
Too well what love women to men may owe.
In faith, they are as true of heart as we.
My father had a daughter loved a man
As it might be, perhaps, were I a woman,
I should your Lordship. 120
ORSINO   And what's her history?

123. **worm i' th' bud:** i.e., a cankerworm inside a rosebud

124. **damask:** pink, rosy

129. **shows . . . will:** outer expressions are larger than actual desires; **still:** always

137. **give no place:** give way to no one; **bide no denay:** accept no denial

2.5 Maria lays her trap for Malvolio by placing her forged letter in his path. From their hiding place, Toby, Andrew, and Fabian observe Malvolio's delight in discovering the love letter. Malvolio promises to obey the letter: to smile, to put on yellow stockings cross-gartered, and to be haughty to Sir Toby. Delighted with their success, Maria and the others prepare to enjoy Malvolio's downfall.

---

1. **Come thy ways:** i.e., come along
2. **scruple:** i.e., tiny amount
5. **sheep-biter:** i.e., dog (Thomas Nashe, in his *An Almond for a Parrat*, 1590, uses the term to describe a hypocritical puritan.)
7. **bearbaiting:** See note to 1.3.93.

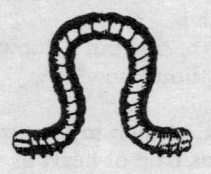

A cankerworm. (2.4.123)
From John Johnstone, *Opera aliquot* . . . (1650–62).

VIOLA
  A blank, my lord. She never told her love,
  But let concealment, like a worm i' th' bud,
  Feed on her damask cheek. She pined in thought,
  And with a green and yellow melancholy   125
  She sat like Patience on a monument,
  Smiling at grief. Was not this love indeed?
  We men may say more, swear more, but indeed
  Our shows are more than will; for still we prove
  Much in our vows but little in our love.   130

ORSINO
  But died thy sister of her love, my boy?

VIOLA
  I am all the daughters of my father's house,
  And all the brothers, too—and yet I know not.
  Sir, shall I to this lady?

ORSINO   Ay, that's the theme.   135
  To her in haste. Give her this jewel. Say
  My love can give no place, bide no denay.
    ⌜*He hands her a jewel and*⌝ *they exit.*

Scene 5
Enter Sir Toby, Sir Andrew, and Fabian.

TOBY Come thy ways, Signior Fabian.

FABIAN Nay, I'll come. If I lose a scruple of this sport, let me be boiled to death with melancholy.

TOBY Wouldst thou not be glad to have the niggardly rascally sheep-biter come by some notable shame?   5

FABIAN I would exult, man. You know he brought me out o' favor with my lady about a bearbaiting here.

TOBY To anger him, we'll have the bear again, and we will fool him black and blue, shall we not, Sir Andrew?   10

ANDREW An we do not, it is pity of our lives.

12. **villain:** here, a term of affection
13. **metal of India:** i.e., golden one (an allusion to the Americas, source of gold in Shakespeare's day)
14. **boxtree:** boxwood shrubbery
19. **Close:** i.e., stay hidden
21. **trout . . . tickling: Trout** can be lured from hiding places by stroking the gills. Here, Malvolio will be "stroked" with flattery.
23. **she did affect me:** i.e., Olivia loved me
24. **come . . . near:** i.e., say something close to this; **fancy:** fall in love
25. **complexion:** nature, appearance
26. **follows:** serves
29. **Contemplation:** anticipation, expectation
30–31. **jets . . . plumes:** struts (like a **turkeycock**) with his feathers spread
32. **'Slight:** By God's light (a strong oath)
36. **Pistol:** i.e., shoot
38–39. **The lady . . . wardrobe:** probably a topical allusion, now lost **yeoman:** servant, officer
40. **Jezebel:** a proud queen in the Bible
41. **deeply in:** i.e., mired in his fantasy
42. **blows:** swells

Enter Maria.

TOBY Here comes the little villain.—How now, my metal of India?

MARIA Get you all three into the boxtree. Malvolio's coming down this walk. He has been yonder i' the sun practicing behavior to his own shadow this half hour. Observe him, for the love of mockery, for I know this letter will make a contemplative idiot of him. Close, in the name of jesting! ⌈*They hide.*⌉ Lie thou there ⌈*putting down the letter,*⌉ for here comes the trout that must be caught with tickling.

She exits.

Enter Malvolio.

MALVOLIO 'Tis but fortune, all is fortune. Maria once told me she did affect me, and I have heard herself come thus near, that should she fancy, it should be one of my complexion. Besides, she uses me with a more exalted respect than anyone else that follows her. What should I think on 't?

TOBY, ⌈*aside*⌉ Here's an overweening rogue.

FABIAN, ⌈*aside*⌉ O, peace! Contemplation makes a rare turkeycock of him. How he jets under his advanced plumes!

ANDREW, ⌈*aside*⌉ 'Slight, I could so beat the rogue!

TOBY, ⌈*aside*⌉ Peace, I say.

MALVOLIO To be Count Malvolio.

TOBY, ⌈*aside*⌉ Ah, rogue!

ANDREW, ⌈*aside*⌉ Pistol him, pistol him!

TOBY, ⌈*aside*⌉ Peace, peace!

MALVOLIO There is example for 't. The lady of the Strachy married the yeoman of the wardrobe.

ANDREW, ⌈*aside*⌉ Fie on him, Jezebel!

FABIAN, ⌈*aside*⌉ O, peace, now he's deeply in. Look how imagination blows him.

44. **state:** i.e., chair of state (as Count Malvolio)
45. **stone-bow:** a crossbow that propels stones
46. **officers:** underlings who manage the estate
47. **branched:** perhaps, embroidered with flowers
51. **have . . . state:** assume a haughty manner fitting my position
52. **a demure . . . regard:** perhaps, soberly surveying my officers
54. **Toby:** Malvolio drops Sir Toby's title, here and in the lines that follow.
62–63. **drawn . . . cars:** i.e., forced from us through torture **cars:** chariots
65–66. **regard of control:** look of mastery
67. **take . . . o':** i.e., give you a blow on
75–76. **break . . . plot:** i.e., cripple, destroy, our scheme

A stone-bow. (2.5.45)
From Jan van der Straet, *Venationes ferarum, auium . . .*
(ca. 1630?)

MALVOLIO Having been three months married to her, sitting in my state—

TOBY, ⌜*aside*⌝ O, for a stone-bow, to hit him in the eye!

MALVOLIO Calling my officers about me, in my branched velvet gown, having come from a daybed, where I have left Olivia sleeping—

TOBY, ⌜*aside*⌝ Fire and brimstone!

FABIAN, ⌜*aside*⌝ O, peace, peace!

MALVOLIO And then to have the humor of state; and after a demure travel of regard, telling them I know my place, as I would they should do theirs, to ask for my kinsman Toby—

TOBY, ⌜*aside*⌝ Bolts and shackles!

FABIAN, ⌜*aside*⌝ O, peace, peace, peace! Now, now.

MALVOLIO Seven of my people, with an obedient start, make out for him. I frown the while, and perchance wind up my watch, or play with my—some rich jewel. Toby approaches; curtsies there to me—

TOBY, ⌜*aside*⌝ Shall this fellow live?

FABIAN, ⌜*aside*⌝ Though our silence be drawn from us with cars, yet peace.

MALVOLIO I extend my hand to him thus, quenching my familiar smile with an austere regard of control—

TOBY, ⌜*aside*⌝ And does not Toby take you a blow o' the lips then?

MALVOLIO Saying "Cousin Toby, my fortunes, having cast me on your niece, give me this prerogative of speech—"

TOBY, ⌜*aside*⌝ What, what?

MALVOLIO "You must amend your drunkenness."

TOBY, ⌜*aside*⌝ Out, scab!

FABIAN, ⌜*aside*⌝ Nay, patience, or we break the sinews of our plot.

MALVOLIO "Besides, you waste the treasure of your time with a foolish knight—"

83. **employment:** i.e., business
85. **woodcock:** a proverbially stupid bird; **gin:** trap (See page 150.)
86. **spirit of humors:** i.e., that which controls moods
86–87. **intimate . . . him:** i.e., suggest to him that he read aloud
89. **hand:** handwriting
89–90. **c's . . . u's . . . t's:** Some editors believe that Shakespeare's audience would have heard a bawdy joke in these lines. They argue that "cut" was a word for the pudendum. Evidence that the word had this meaning is, however, far from conclusive.
90–91. **in contempt of question:** i.e., without a doubt
94. **By your leave:** i.e., with your permission (Malvolio's apology to the wax seal before he breaks it)
95. **impressure:** image stamped on the wax; **Lucrece:** i.e., a picture of the chaste Lucretia, whose story Shakespeare had told in *The Rape of Lucrece* (See page 170.)
96. **uses to seal:** is accustomed to sealing
103. **numbers:** meter
106. **brock:** a term of contempt (literally, badger)
108. **Lucrece knife:** Lucretia stabbed herself after being raped by Tarquin. (See note on line 95 above.)
110. **sway:** rule
111. **fustian:** pretentious, pompous
112. **Excellent wench:** i.e., Maria

ANDREW, ⌜*aside*⌝ That's me, I warrant you.
MALVOLIO "One Sir Andrew."
ANDREW, ⌜*aside*⌝ I knew 'twas I, for many do call me fool.
MALVOLIO, ⌜*seeing the letter*⌝ What employment have we here?
FABIAN, ⌜*aside*⌝ Now is the woodcock near the gin.
TOBY, ⌜*aside*⌝ O, peace, and the spirit of humors intimate reading aloud to him.
MALVOLIO, ⌜*taking up the letter*⌝ By my life, this is my lady's hand! These be her very *c*'s, her *u*'s, and her *t*'s, and thus makes she her great *P*'s. It is in contempt of question her hand.
ANDREW, ⌜*aside*⌝ Her *c*'s, her *u*'s, and her *t*'s. Why that?
MALVOLIO ⌜*reads*⌝ *To the unknown beloved, this, and my good wishes*—Her very phrases! By your leave, wax. Soft. And the impressure her Lucrece, with which she uses to seal—'tis my lady! ⌜*He opens the letter.*⌝ To whom should this be?
FABIAN, ⌜*aside*⌝ This wins him, liver and all.
MALVOLIO ⌜*reads*⌝

> *Jove knows I love,*
> *But who?*
> *Lips, do not move;*
> *No man must know.*

"No man must know." What follows? The numbers altered. "No man must know." If this should be thee, Malvolio!
TOBY, ⌜*aside*⌝ Marry, hang thee, brock!
MALVOLIO ⌜*reads*⌝

> *I may command where I adore,*
> *But silence, like a Lucrece knife,*
> *With bloodless stroke my heart doth gore;*
> *M.O.A.I. doth sway my life.*

FABIAN, ⌜*aside*⌝ A fustian riddle!
TOBY, ⌜*aside*⌝ Excellent wench, say I.

115. **What dish:** i.e., what a dish; **dressed:** prepared for

117. **staniel:** an inferior kind of hawk

117–18. **checks at it:** turns to follow it

121. **formal capacity:** i.e., sane mind

122. **obstruction:** difficulty

125. **make up:** i.e., make sense out of

125–26. **He . . . scent:** i.e., he's like a hound who has lost the trail of his quarry (Language describing Malvolio as a dog following a scent continues in lines 127–28, where **Sowter** seems to be the dog's name and **cry upon 't** means "bark loudly," and in line 132, where **fault** is a technical term for a lost scent. See page 114.)

128. **rank:** strong smelling

133–34. **no consonancy . . . sequel:** i.e., no harmony in the letters that follow (See note about Malvolio's language at 2.3.91–92.)

134. **suffers under probation:** i.e., stands up to testing

143–44. **This simulation . . . former:** i.e., this part of the letter does not resemble me as clearly as does the first part ("I may command where I adore")

147. **revolve:** consider

148. **stars:** i.e., destiny

MALVOLIO "M.O.A.I. doth sway my life." Nay, but first let me see, let me see, let me see.

FABIAN, ⌜aside⌝ What dish o' poison has she dressed him!

TOBY, ⌜aside⌝ And with what wing the ⌜staniel⌝ checks at it!

MALVOLIO "I may command where I adore." Why, she may command me; I serve her, she is my lady. Why, this is evident to any formal capacity. There is no obstruction in this. And the end—what should that alphabetical position portend? If I could make that resemble something in me! Softly! "M.O.A.I."—

TOBY, ⌜aside⌝ O, ay, make up that.—He is now at a cold scent.

FABIAN, ⌜aside⌝ Sowter will cry upon 't for all this, though it be as rank as a fox.

MALVOLIO "M"—Malvolio. "M"—why, that begins my name!

FABIAN, ⌜aside⌝ Did not I say he would work it out? The cur is excellent at faults.

MALVOLIO "M." But then there is no consonancy in the sequel that suffers under probation. "A" should follow, but "O" does.

FABIAN, ⌜aside⌝ And "O" shall end, I hope.

TOBY, ⌜aside⌝ Ay, or I'll cudgel him and make him cry "O."

MALVOLIO And then "I" comes behind.

FABIAN, ⌜aside⌝ Ay, an you had any eye behind you, you might see more detraction at your heels than fortunes before you.

MALVOLIO "M.O.A.I." This simulation is not as the former, and yet to crush this a little, it would bow to me, for every one of these letters are in my name. Soft, here follows prose.
⌜He reads.⌝ *If this fall into thy hand, revolve. In my stars I am above thee, but be not afraid of greatness.*

150–51. **open their hands:** i.e., have become generous

152. **inure:** accustom; **like:** likely

152–53. **cast . . . slough:** discard your humble attitude (as a snake discards its old skin)

153. **opposite:** confrontational

154–55. **tang . . . state:** ring out with political opinions

155–56. **Put . . . singularity:** i.e., adopt idiosyncrasies

158. **cross-gartered:** wearing ribbons tied around the knees (See pages 86 and 112.)

159. **Go to:** an expression of protest (like "Come, come")

164. **champian:** open country; **discovers:** reveals

165. **open:** perfectly clear; **politic:** (1) political; (2) wise

166. **baffle:** publicly humiliate; **gross:** base

167. **point-devise . . . man:** i.e., precisely the man described in the letter

168. **jade:** dupe, delude

173. **these . . . liking:** i.e., wear the kind of clothes that she likes

174. **strange:** extraordinary, exceptional; **stout:** proud, arrogant

179. **thou entertain'st:** you accept

Some are ⌜born⌝ great, some ⌜achieve⌝ greatness, and some have greatness thrust upon 'em. Thy fates open their hands. Let thy blood and spirit embrace them. And, to inure thyself to what thou art like to be, cast thy humble slough and appear fresh. Be opposite with a kinsman, surly with servants. Let thy tongue tang arguments of state. Put thyself into the trick of singularity. She thus advises thee that sighs for thee. Remember who commended thy yellow stockings and wished to see thee ever cross-gartered. I say, remember. Go to, thou art made, if thou desir'st to be so. If not, let me see thee a steward still, the fellow of servants, and not worthy to touch Fortune's fingers. Farewell. She that would alter services with thee,
      The Fortunate-Unhappy.

Daylight and champian discovers not more! This is open. I will be proud, I will read politic authors, I will baffle Sir Toby, I will wash off gross acquaintance, I will be point-devise the very man. I do not now fool myself, to let imagination jade me; for every reason excites to this, that my lady loves me. She did commend my yellow stockings of late, she did praise my leg being cross-gartered, and in this she manifests herself to my love and, with a kind of injunction, drives me to these habits of her liking. I thank my stars, I am happy. I will be strange, stout, in yellow stockings, and cross-gartered, even with the swiftness of putting on. Jove and my stars be praised! Here is yet a postscript.
⌜*He reads.*⌝ *Thou canst not choose but know who I am. If thou entertain'st my love, let it appear in thy smiling; thy smiles become thee well. Therefore in my presence still smile, dear my sweet, I prithee.*
Jove, I thank thee! I will smile. I will do everything that thou wilt have me.   *He exits.*

185. **Sophy:** shah of Persia
191. **gull-catcher:** A *gull* is a person easily cheated.
194. **play:** bet; **tray-trip:** a gambling game
200. **aqua vitae:** strong drink, usually brandy
208. **notable contempt:** i.e., well-known object of contempt
210. **Tartar:** i.e., Tartarus, hell
212. **make one, too:** i.e., join you

Legs cross-gartered. (2.5.158)
From Abraham de Bruyn, *Omnium pene Europae, Asiae . . . gentium habitus . . .* (1581).

FABIAN I will not give my part of this sport for a pension of thousands to be paid from the Sophy.
TOBY I could marry this wench for this device.
ANDREW So could I, too.
TOBY And ask no other dowry with her but such another jest.
ANDREW Nor I neither.

Enter Maria.

FABIAN Here comes my noble gull-catcher.
TOBY Wilt thou set thy foot o' my neck?
ANDREW Or o' mine either?
TOBY Shall I play my freedom at tray-trip and become thy bondslave?
ANDREW I' faith, or I either?
TOBY Why, thou hast put him in such a dream that when the image of it leaves him he must run mad.
MARIA Nay, but say true, does it work upon him?
TOBY Like aqua vitae with a midwife.
MARIA If you will then see the fruits of the sport, mark his first approach before my lady. He will come to her in yellow stockings, and 'tis a color she abhors, and cross-gartered, a fashion she detests; and he will smile upon her, which will now be so unsuitable to her disposition, being addicted to a melancholy as she is, that it cannot but turn him into a notable contempt. If you will see it, follow me.
TOBY To the gates of Tartar, thou most excellent devil of wit!
ANDREW I'll make one, too.

They exit.

TWELFTH NIGHT,
OR,
WHAT YOU WILL

ACT 3

3.1 Viola (as Cesario), on her way to see Olivia, encounters first the Fool and then Sir Toby and Sir Andrew. Olivia, meeting Cesario, sends the others away and declares her love.

---

0 SD. **tabor:** small drum

1. **Save thee:** i.e., God save thee (a friendly greeting)

1–2. **Dost thou live by:** i.e., do you make your living by playing

4. **churchman:** clergyman

5. **No such matter:** i.e., not at all

11. **You have said:** i.e., you're right; **this age:** i.e., the age in which we live

12. **chev'ril:** kid leather, which stretches easily

14. **dally nicely:** play with precise meanings (**Dally** also means "flirt, play with amorously.")

15. **wanton:** changeable, ambiguous (also "immoral, unchaste")

21. **bonds:** i.e., the legal requirement that one's pledge (**word**) be backed by a written contract, or **bond**

ACT 3

Scene 1
Enter Viola and ⌜Feste, the Fool, playing a tabor.⌝

VIOLA Save thee, friend, and thy music. Dost thou live by thy tabor?
FOOL No, sir, I live by the church.
VIOLA Art thou a churchman?
FOOL No such matter, sir. I do live by the church, for I do live at my house, and my house doth stand by the church.
VIOLA So thou mayst say the ⌜king⌝ lies by a beggar if a beggar dwell near him, or the church stands by thy tabor if thy tabor stand by the church.
FOOL You have said, sir. To see this age! A sentence is but a chev'ril glove to a good wit. How quickly the wrong side may be turned outward!
VIOLA Nay, that's certain. They that dally nicely with words may quickly make them wanton.
FOOL I would therefore my sister had had no name, sir.
VIOLA Why, man?
FOOL Why, sir, her name's a word, and to dally with that word might make my sister wanton. But, indeed, words are very rascals since bonds disgraced them.
VIOLA Thy reason, man?

27. **I warrant:** i.e., I'm sure

36. **pilchers:** pilchards, small fish related to the herring

39. **late:** lately, recently

40. **walk . . . orb:** move around the earth

41–42. **but . . . be:** i.e., unless the Fool were

43. **your Wisdom:** an ironic title (analogous to "your Honor")

44. **an thou . . . me:** i.e., if you attack me; **I'll no more:** i.e., I'll have no more to do

46. **in . . . commodity:** i.e., out of his next supply

51. **Would . . . bred:** The Fool, begging for money, suggests that money can breed, i.e., reproduce. Viola continues the wordplay in her response, where **put to use** means "invested to earn interest," but also has a sexual meaning.

53–54. **Lord . . . Troilus:** The allusion is to the story of Troilus and Cressida, lovers who were brought together by Pandarus. The story was told by Chaucer, and by Shakespeare in his *Troilus and Cressida*.

57. **Cressida . . . beggar:** In some versions of the story, Cressida becomes a beggar before her death.

FOOL   Troth, sir, I can yield you none without words, and words are grown so false I am loath to prove reason with them.
VIOLA   I warrant thou art a merry fellow and car'st for nothing.
FOOL   Not so, sir. I do care for something. But in my conscience, sir, I do not care for you. If that be to care for nothing, sir, I would it would make you invisible.
VIOLA   Art not thou the Lady Olivia's Fool?
FOOL   No, indeed, sir. The Lady Olivia has no folly. She will keep no Fool, sir, till she be married, and Fools are as like husbands as pilchers are to herrings: the husband's the bigger. I am indeed not her Fool but her corrupter of words.
VIOLA   I saw thee late at the Count Orsino's.
FOOL   Foolery, sir, does walk about the orb like the sun; it shines everywhere. I would be sorry, sir, but the Fool should be as oft with your master as with my mistress. I think I saw your Wisdom there.
VIOLA   Nay, an thou pass upon me, I'll no more with thee. Hold, there's expenses for thee. ⌜*Giving a coin.*⌝
FOOL   Now Jove, in his next commodity of hair, send thee a beard!
VIOLA   By my troth I'll tell thee, I am almost sick for one, ⌜*aside*⌝ though I would not have it grow on my chin.—Is thy lady within?
FOOL   Would not a pair of these have bred, sir?
VIOLA   Yes, being kept together and put to use.
FOOL   I would play Lord Pandarus of Phrygia, sir, to bring a Cressida to this Troilus.
VIOLA   I understand you, sir. 'Tis well begged. ⌜*Giving another coin.*⌝
FOOL   The matter I hope is not great, sir, begging but a beggar: Cressida was a beggar. My lady is within, sir.

58. **conster to them:** i.e., construe (explain) to those in the house

59. **out ... welkin:** i.e., beyond my comprehension, out of my element (The wordplay here is on **welkin** as "sky," which, as "air," is an **element**.)

64. **quality:** rank; nature

65. **haggard:** wild hawk; **check at:** turn to follow

66. **practice:** profession

67. **art:** learning, skill

68. **fit:** i.e., fitting, appropriate

69. **wit:** intelligence (or reputation for it)

72. **Dieu ... monsieur:** God save you, sir.

73. **Et ... serviteur!:** And you as well, your servant!

75. **encounter:** i.e., approach (Toby uses affected language, and Viola answers him in kind.)

78. **list:** limit, boundary

80. **understand:** i.e., stand under, hold me up

84. **with ... entrance:** i.e., by going and entering

85. **we are prevented:** i.e., Olivia's appearance anticipates our entrance

I will conster to them whence you come. Who you are and what you would are out of my welkin—I might say "element," but the word is overworn.
He exits.

VIOLA
This fellow is wise enough to play the Fool,
And to do that well craves a kind of wit.
He must observe their mood on whom he jests,
The quality of persons, and the time,
And, like the haggard, check at every feather
That comes before his eye. This is a practice
As full of labor as a wise man's art:
For folly that he wisely shows is fit;
But ⌜wise men,⌝ folly-fall'n, quite taint their wit.

Enter Sir Toby and Andrew.

TOBY Save you, gentleman.
VIOLA And you, sir.
ANDREW *Dieu vous garde, monsieur.*
VIOLA *Et vous aussi. Votre serviteur!*
ANDREW I hope, sir, you are, and I am yours.
TOBY Will you encounter the house? My niece is desirous you should enter, if your trade be to her.
VIOLA I am bound to your niece, sir; I mean, she is the list of my voyage.
TOBY Taste your legs, sir; put them to motion.
VIOLA My legs do better understand me, sir, than I understand what you mean by bidding me taste my legs.
TOBY I mean, to go, sir, to enter.
VIOLA I will answer you with gait and entrance—but we are prevented.

Enter Olivia, and ⌜Maria, her⌝ Gentlewoman.

Most excellent accomplished lady, the heavens rain odors on you!

90. **My . . . but:** i.e., my message cannot be spoken except

91. **pregnant:** receptive; **vouchsafed:** willing, graciously attentive

101. **lowly feigning:** i.e., pretending to be humble; **was called:** i.e., began to be considered

105. **For:** as for; **on him:** i.e., about him

113. **music . . . spheres:** In Ptolemaic astronomy, the stars move about the earth in crystalline spheres, giving out incredibly beautiful music that humans cannot hear.

115. **Give . . . you:** i.e., permit me to speak, I beg you

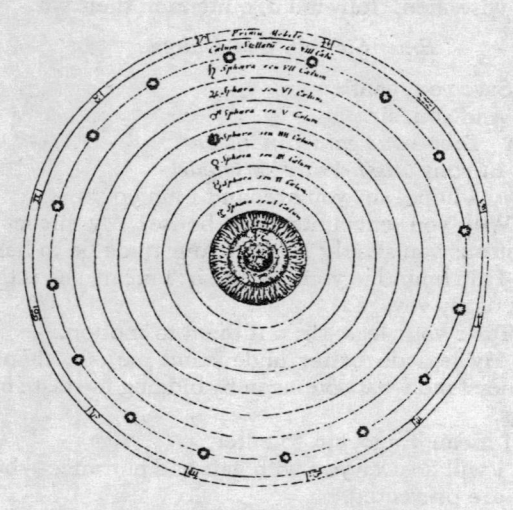

Ptolemaic universe. (3.1.113)
From Marcus Manilius, *The sphere of . . .* (1675)

ANDREW, ⌐aside⌐ That youth's a rare courtier. "Rain odors," well.

VIOLA My matter hath no voice, lady, but to your own most pregnant and vouchsafed ear.

ANDREW, ⌐aside⌐ "Odors," "pregnant," and "vouchsafed." I'll get 'em all three all ready.

OLIVIA Let the garden door be shut, and leave me to my hearing. ⌐*Sir Toby, Sir Andrew, and Maria exit.*⌐ Give me your hand, sir.

VIOLA
My duty, madam, and most humble service.

OLIVIA What is your name?

VIOLA
Cesario is your servant's name, fair princess.

OLIVIA
My servant, sir? 'Twas never merry world
Since lowly feigning was called compliment.
You're servant to the Count Orsino, youth.

VIOLA
And he is yours, and his must needs be yours.
Your servant's servant is your servant, madam.

OLIVIA
For him, I think not on him. For his thoughts,
Would they were blanks rather than filled with me.

VIOLA
Madam, I come to whet your gentle thoughts
On his behalf.

OLIVIA O, by your leave, I pray you.
I bade you never speak again of him.
But would you undertake another suit,
I had rather hear you to solicit that
Than music from the spheres.

VIOLA Dear lady—

OLIVIA
Give me leave, beseech you. I did send,
After the last enchantment you did here,

117. **abuse:** deceive; wrong

119–21. **Under . . . yours:** i.e., I must be judged harshly by you, since I used shameful cunning to force on you something you knew was not yours

123–25. **Have . . . think:** The image here is of a bearbaiting. Olivia imagines her honor as a bear tied to the stake, attacked (**baited**) by the **unmuzzled** dogs that are Cesario's **thoughts.**

127. **cypress:** thin (almost transparent) cloth veil

130, 131. **degree, grize:** step

131. **a . . . proof:** an ordinary experience

140. **proper:** handsome

142. **westward ho!:** the cry of Thames watermen headed from London to Westminster

144. **You'll nothing . . . ?:** i.e., you have no message . . . ?

A bearbaiting. (1.3.93)
From Franco Giacomo, *Habiti d'huomeni de donne Venetiane . . .* (1609?).

A ring in chase of you. So did I abuse
Myself, my servant, and, I fear me, you.
Under your hard construction must I sit,
To force that on you in a shameful cunning
Which you knew none of yours. What might you think?
Have you not set mine honor at the stake,
And baited it with all th' unmuzzled thoughts
That tyrannous heart can think? To one of your receiving
Enough is shown. A cypress, not a bosom,
Hides my heart. So, let me hear you speak.

VIOLA
I pity you.

OLIVIA   That's a degree to love.

VIOLA
No, not a grize, for 'tis a vulgar proof
That very oft we pity enemies.

OLIVIA
Why then methinks 'tis time to smile again.
O world, how apt the poor are to be proud!
If one should be a prey, how much the better
To fall before the lion than the wolf.   *Clock strikes.*
The clock upbraids me with the waste of time.
Be not afraid, good youth, I will not have you.
And yet when wit and youth is come to harvest,
Your wife is like to reap a proper man.
There lies your way, due west.

VIOLA   Then westward ho!
Grace and good disposition attend your Ladyship.
You'll nothing, madam, to my lord by me?

OLIVIA
Stay. I prithee, tell me what thou think'st of me.

VIOLA
That you do think you are not what you are.

148. **think you right:** i.e., you think correctly

155–56. **Love's . . . noon:** i.e., love cannot be hidden

159. **maugre . . . pride:** i.e., despite your scorn

160. **Nor . . . nor:** neither . . . nor

161. **extort thy reasons:** i.e., force out excuses; **clause:** premise

162. **For . . . cause:** i.e., because I am the wooer, you have no cause (to woo me)

163. **reason . . . fetter:** i.e., restrain such rationalizing by considering the following sentence

167. **nor never none:** nor anyone ever

Cupid with his bow. (1.1.37)
From Johannes ab Indigane, *The booke of palmestry* (1666).

OLIVIA
If I think so, I think the same of you.
VIOLA
Then think you right. I am not what I am.
OLIVIA
I would you were as I would have you be.
VIOLA
Would it be better, madam, than I am? 150
I wish it might, for now I am your fool.
OLIVIA, ⌈*aside*⌉
O, what a deal of scorn looks beautiful
In the contempt and anger of his lip!
A murd'rous guilt shows not itself more soon
Than love that would seem hid. Love's night is 155
    noon.—
Cesario, by the roses of the spring,
By maidhood, honor, truth, and everything,
I love thee so, that, maugre all thy pride,
Nor wit nor reason can my passion hide. 160
Do not extort thy reasons from this clause,
For that I woo, thou therefore hast no cause;
But rather reason thus with reason fetter:
Love sought is good, but given unsought is better.
VIOLA
By innocence I swear, and by my youth, 165
I have one heart, one bosom, and one truth,
And that no woman has, nor never none
Shall mistress be of it, save I alone.
And so adieu, good madam. Nevermore
Will I my master's tears to you deplore. 170
OLIVIA
Yet come again, for thou perhaps mayst move
That heart, which now abhors, to like his love.
                They exit ⌈*in different directions.*⌉

3.2 Sir Andrew, convinced that Olivia will never love him, threatens to leave. Sir Toby persuades him that he can win her love if he challenges Cesario to a duel. Sir Andrew goes off to prepare a letter for Cesario. Maria enters to say that Malvolio has followed every point in the letter and is about to incur disaster when he appears before Olivia.

---

3. **must needs yield:** i.e., must give
6. **orchard:** garden
10. **argument:** token, evidence
13. **prove it legitimate:** i.e., make good my case; **oaths of:** i.e., testimony sworn under oath by
15. **they:** i.e., judgment and reason; **grand-jurymen:** those who decide whether there is sufficient evidence to bring a case to trial
18. **dormouse:** i.e., sleeping (The **dormouse** becomes torpid in cold weather. See page 172.)
23. **at your hand:** i.e., from you
24. **balked:** passed up, neglected; **gilt:** gold plating (Fabian plays with the idea of a missed "golden **opportunity**.")
25–26. **sailed . . . opinion:** i.e., earned my lady's cold regard
29. **policy:** statesmanlike wisdom (Andrew, in his response, gives the word its meaning of "political cunning.")
31. **as lief:** i.e., just as soon; **Brownist:** a believer in the then-revolutionary ideas about religion preached by Robert Browne (c.1550–1633)
33. **build me:** i.e., build

Scene 2
Enter Sir Toby, Sir Andrew, and Fabian.

ANDREW No, faith, I'll not stay a jot longer.

TOBY Thy reason, dear venom, give thy reason.

FABIAN You must needs yield your reason, Sir Andrew.

ANDREW Marry, I saw your niece do more favors to the Count's servingman than ever she bestowed upon me. I saw 't i' th' orchard.

TOBY Did she see ⌜thee⌝ the while, old boy? Tell me that.

ANDREW As plain as I see you now.

FABIAN This was a great argument of love in her toward you.

ANDREW 'Slight, will you make an ass o' me?

FABIAN I will prove it legitimate, sir, upon the oaths of judgment and reason.

TOBY And they have been grand-jurymen since before Noah was a sailor.

FABIAN She did show favor to the youth in your sight only to exasperate you, to awake your dormouse valor, to put fire in your heart and brimstone in your liver. You should then have accosted her, and with some excellent jests, fire-new from the mint, you should have banged the youth into dumbness. This was looked for at your hand, and this was balked. The double gilt of this opportunity you let time wash off, and you are now sailed into the north of my lady's opinion, where you will hang like an icicle on a Dutchman's beard, unless you do redeem it by some laudable attempt either of valor or policy.

ANDREW An 't be any way, it must be with valor, for policy I hate. I had as lief be a Brownist as a politician.

TOBY Why, then, build me thy fortunes upon the basis

34. **Challenge me:** i.e., challenge
37. **love-broker:** go-between
41. **curst:** fierce, savage
42. **so it be:** i.e., as long as it is
43. **invention:** arguments; inventiveness
43–44. **with . . . ink:** i.e., with the freedom given to one who puts his challenge in writing
44. **"thou"-est . . . thrice:** i.e., address him three times as "thou" instead of "you" (The use of the familiar "thou" to a stranger would be an insult.)
47. **bed of Ware:** a famous ten-foot-wide bed (now in a museum in London)
48. **gall:** (1) oak galls, used in making ink; (2) bitterness
49. **goose-pen:** (1) a pen made with a goose quill; (2) a pen used by a goose (i.e., a fool)
51. **cubiculo:** bedchamber
52. **dear manikin:** i.e., valued little man (**Manikin** is a term of contempt.)
53. **dear:** expensive, costly
58. **wainropes:** i.e., wagon ropes
59. **hale:** haul, pull, drag
60. **blood . . . liver:** Cowards were supposed to have white or bloodless livers.
62. **anatomy:** i.e., the body being dissected
63. **opposite:** rival
66. **desire the spleen:** i.e., want to laugh

of valor. Challenge me the Count's youth to fight with him. Hurt him in eleven places. My niece shall take note of it, and assure thyself, there is no love-broker in the world can more prevail in man's commendation with woman than report of valor.

FABIAN There is no way but this, Sir Andrew.

ANDREW Will either of you bear me a challenge to him?

TOBY Go, write it in a martial hand. Be curst and brief. It is no matter how witty, so it be eloquent and full of invention. Taunt him with the license of ink. If thou "thou"-est him some thrice, it shall not be amiss, and as many lies as will lie in thy sheet of paper, although the sheet were big enough for the bed of Ware in England, set 'em down. Go, about it. Let there be gall enough in thy ink, though thou write with a goose-pen, no matter. About it.

ANDREW Where shall I find you?

TOBY We'll call thee at the cubiculo. Go.

Sir Andrew exits.

FABIAN This is a dear manikin to you, Sir Toby.

TOBY I have been dear to him, lad, some two thousand strong, or so.

FABIAN We shall have a rare letter from him. But you'll not deliver 't?

TOBY Never trust me, then. And by all means stir on the youth to an answer. I think oxen and wainropes cannot hale them together. For Andrew, if he were opened and you find so much blood in his liver as will clog the foot of a flea, I'll eat the rest of th' anatomy.

FABIAN And his opposite, the youth, bears in his visage no great presage of cruelty.

Enter Maria.

TOBY Look where the youngest wren of mine comes.

MARIA If you desire the spleen, and will laugh your-

67. **gull:** dupe
68. **a very renegado:** i.e., no longer a Christian
69. **means:** intends
70. **passages:** acts
73. **villainously:** atrociously; **pedant:** i.e., teacher
77. **new map:** an allusion to a map published in 1599, among the first to use Mercator projection, and thus filled with prominent lines (See page xxxi.)
78. **augmentation . . . Indies:** i.e., more complete mappings of the East Indies

3.3 Antonio, having followed Sebastian, explains the incident in his past that keeps him from safely venturing into the streets of Orsino's city. Giving his money to Sebastian, Antonio sets off to their inn while Sebastian goes off to see the sights.

---

1. **by my will:** i.e., willingly
5. **filèd:** ground to a sharp edge with a file
6. **not all love:** i.e., not only a desire
8. **jealousy:** fear of
9. **skill-less in:** i.e., without knowledge of
12. **The . . . fear:** i.e., spurred by these anxieties

selves into stitches, follow me. Yond gull Malvolio is
turned heathen, a very renegado; for there is no
Christian that means to be saved by believing rightly
can ever believe such impossible passages of grossness. He's in yellow stockings.
TOBY And cross-gartered?
MARIA Most villainously, like a pedant that keeps a
school i' th' church. I have dogged him like his
murderer. He does obey every point of the letter
that I dropped to betray him. He does smile his face
into more lines than is in the new map with the
augmentation of the Indies. You have not seen such
a thing as 'tis. I can hardly forbear hurling things at
him. I know my lady will strike him. If she do, he'll
smile and take 't for a great favor.
TOBY Come, bring us, bring us where he is.

They all exit.

Scene 3
Enter Sebastian and Antonio.

SEBASTIAN
I would not by my will have troubled you,
But, since you make your pleasure of your pains,
I will no further chide you.
ANTONIO
I could not stay behind you. My desire,
More sharp than filèd steel, did spur me forth;
And not all love to see you, though so much
As might have drawn one to a longer voyage,
But jealousy what might befall your travel,
Being skill-less in these parts, which to a stranger,
Unguided and unfriended, often prove
Rough and unhospitable. My willing love,
The rather by these arguments of fear,
Set forth in your pursuit.

16–17. **oft . . . pay:** i.e., good acts are often rewarded with mere words **uncurrent:** not negotiable, worthless

18. **worth:** possessions, wealth; **conscience:** i.e., recognition of obligation (to you)

20. **relics:** i.e., antiquities, old buildings, etc.

25. **renown this city:** i.e., make this city famous

26. **Would . . . me:** i.e., please excuse me

28. **Count his:** Count's

29. **of such note:** i.e., so memorable

30. **it . . . answered:** i.e., I would hardly be able (1) to defend myself before the law, or (2) to endure the penalty exacted from me

31. **Belike:** perhaps

34. **bloody argument:** a reason worth shedding blood for

35. **answered:** recompensed

36. **for traffic's sake:** i.e., for the sake of trade

37. **stood out:** i.e., refused

38. **be lapsèd:** i.e., am caught

39. **dear:** dearly, at great cost

41. **It . . . me:** it is not fitting for me

43. **bespeak:** arrange for; **diet:** meals

108

SEBASTIAN   My kind Antonio,
I can no other answer make but thanks,
And thanks, and ever ⌜thanks; and⌝ oft good turns
Are shuffled off with such uncurrent pay.
But were my worth, as is my conscience, firm,
You should find better dealing. What's to do?
Shall we go see the relics of this town?

ANTONIO
Tomorrow, sir. Best first go see your lodging.

SEBASTIAN
I am not weary, and 'tis long to night.
I pray you, let us satisfy our eyes
With the memorials and the things of fame
That do renown this city.

ANTONIO   Would you'd pardon me.
I do not without danger walk these streets.
Once in a sea fight 'gainst the Count his galleys
I did some service, of such note indeed
That were I ta'en here it would scarce be answered.

SEBASTIAN
Belike you slew great number of his people?

ANTONIO
Th' offense is not of such a bloody nature,
Albeit the quality of the time and quarrel
Might well have given us bloody argument.
It might have since been answered in repaying
What we took from them, which, for traffic's sake,
Most of our city did. Only myself stood out,
For which, if I be lapsèd in this place,
I shall pay dear.

SEBASTIAN   Do not then walk too open.

ANTONIO
It doth not fit me. Hold, sir, here's my purse.
⌜*Giving him money.*⌝
In the south suburbs, at the Elephant,
Is best to lodge. I will bespeak our diet

44. **beguile:** while away
46. **There . . . me:** i.e., you will find me there (at the Elephant)
48. **Haply:** perhaps; **toy:** trifle
49. **store:** supply of money
50. **is . . . markets:** i.e., will not cover whimsical purchases

---

3.4 Malvolio, dressed ridiculously and smiling grotesquely, appears before an astonished Olivia. Thinking him insane, she puts him in the care of Sir Toby, who decides to treat him as a madman by having him bound and put in a dark room. Toby also decides to deliver Sir Andrew's challenge to Cesario in person in order to force the two of them into a duel. Terrified, they prepare to fight. At that moment, Antonio enters, thinks that Cesario is Sebastian, and comes to his defense. Antonio is immediately arrested by Orsino's officers. Since he is sure that Viola is Sebastian, Antonio is bitter about the apparent denial of their friendship. Viola is herself delighted by Antonio's angry words because, since he called her Sebastian, there is hope that her brother may in fact be alive.

---

2. **bestow of:** bestow on, give
6. **sad and civil:** serious-minded and polite
10. **possessed:** i.e., by the devil (This was one popular explanation of insanity.)
11. **rave:** speak incoherently
14. **in 's:** in his
16. **equal be:** i.e., are equal

110

Whiles you beguile the time and feed your
  knowledge
With viewing of the town. There shall you have me.
SEBASTIAN Why I your purse?
ANTONIO
Haply your eye shall light upon some toy
You have desire to purchase, and your store,
I think, is not for idle markets, sir.
SEBASTIAN
I'll be your purse-bearer and leave you
For an hour.
ANTONIO   To th' Elephant.
SEBASTIAN   I do remember.
They exit ⌜in different directions.⌝

Scene 4
Enter Olivia and Maria.

OLIVIA, ⌜*aside*⌝
I have sent after him. He says he'll come.
How shall I feast him? What bestow of him?
For youth is bought more oft than begged or
  borrowed.
I speak too loud.—
Where's Malvolio? He is sad and civil
And suits well for a servant with my fortunes.
Where is Malvolio?
MARIA He's coming, madam, but in very strange manner. He is sure possessed, madam.
OLIVIA Why, what's the matter? Does he rave?
MARIA No, madam, he does nothing but smile. Your Ladyship were best to have some guard about you if he come, for sure the man is tainted in 's wits.
OLIVIA
Go call him hither. ⌜*Maria exits.*⌝ I am as mad as he,
If sad and merry madness equal be.

19. **sad:** serious (Malvolio takes the word to mean "sorrowful.")
24. **sonnet:** song ("Please one, and please all" is the refrain of a ballad about the wishes of women.)
28. **black in my mind:** i.e., melancholy
30–31. **Roman hand:** Italian-style handwriting
33–34. **Ay . . . thee:** a line from a popular song
38–39. **nightingales answer daws:** i.e., fine birds don't respond to the call of crows

Legs cross-gartered. (3.4.23)
From Abraham de Bruyn, *Omnium pene Europae, Asiae . . . gentium habitus . . .* (1581).

Enter ⌜Maria with⌝ Malvolio.

How now, Malvolio?
MALVOLIO   Sweet lady, ho, ho!
OLIVIA Smil'st thou? I sent for thee upon a sad occasion.
MALVOLIO Sad, lady? I could be sad. This does make some obstruction in the blood, this cross-gartering, but what of that? If it please the eye of one, it is with me as the very true sonnet is: "Please one, and please all."
⌜OLIVIA⌝ Why, how dost thou, man? What is the matter with thee?
MALVOLIO Not black in my mind, though yellow in my legs. It did come to his hands, and commands shall be executed. I think we do know the sweet Roman hand.
OLIVIA Wilt thou go to bed, Malvolio?
MALVOLIO To bed? "Ay, sweetheart, and I'll come to thee."
OLIVIA God comfort thee! Why dost thou smile so, and kiss thy hand so oft?
MARIA How do you, Malvolio?
MALVOLIO At your request? Yes, nightingales answer daws!
MARIA Why appear you with this ridiculous boldness before my lady?
MALVOLIO "Be not afraid of greatness." 'Twas well writ.
OLIVIA What mean'st thou by that, Malvolio?
MALVOLIO "Some are born great—"
OLIVIA Ha?
MALVOLIO "Some achieve greatness—"
OLIVIA What sayst thou?
MALVOLIO "And some have greatness thrust upon them."

61. **very:** genuine, true; **midsummer madness:** insanity (The midsummer moon was thought to cause madness.)

63. **hardly:** i.e., only with great difficulty

68. **miscarry:** come to harm

78. **consequently:** i.e., subsequently, later

79–80. **in . . . note:** i.e., dressed like some noteworthy gentleman

80. **limed:** trapped, as with birdlime

81. **it is Jove's doing:** a possible allusion to Psalm 188.23, "This is the Lord's doing." (The names "God" and "Jove" are used almost interchangeably in this play.)

82. **fellow:** used dismissively by Olivia but heard by Malvolio as meaning "companion"

A hound on the scent. (2.5.125–32)
From George Turbeville, *The noble arte of venerie* (1611).

OLIVIA Heaven restore thee!
MALVOLIO "Remember who commended thy yellow stockings—"
OLIVIA Thy yellow stockings?
MALVOLIO "And wished to see thee cross-gartered." 55
OLIVIA Cross-gartered?
MALVOLIO "Go to, thou art made, if thou desir'st to be so—"
OLIVIA Am I made?
MALVOLIO "If not, let me see thee a servant still." 60
OLIVIA Why, this is very midsummer madness!

Enter Servant.

SERVANT Madam, the young gentleman of the Count Orsino's is returned. I could hardly entreat him back. He attends your Ladyship's pleasure.
OLIVIA I'll come to him. ⌜*Servant exits.*⌝ Good Maria, let 65
this fellow be looked to. Where's my Cousin Toby? Let some of my people have a special care of him. I would not have him miscarry for the half of my dowry.
⌜*Olivia and Maria*⌝ *exit* ⌜*in different directions.*⌝
MALVOLIO O ho, do you come near me now? No worse 70
man than Sir Toby to look to me. This concurs directly with the letter. She sends him on purpose that I may appear stubborn to him, for she incites me to that in the letter: "Cast thy humble slough," says she. "Be opposite with a kinsman, surly with 75
servants; let thy tongue ⌜tang⌝ with arguments of state; put thyself into the trick of singularity," and consequently sets down the manner how: as, a sad face, a reverend carriage, a slow tongue, in the habit of some Sir of note, and so forth. I have limed her, 80
but it is Jove's doing, and Jove make me thankful! And when she went away now, "Let this fellow be looked to." "Fellow!" Not "Malvolio," nor after my

84. **degree:** i.e., my rank as her steward

84–85. **adheres together:** i.e., coheres, fits

85. **dram:** tiniest bit (literally, an apothecaries' weight of 60 grains); **scruple:** doubt (also, an apothecaries' weight of 20 grains)

86. **incredulous:** incredible; **unsafe:** unreliable, untrustworthy

92. **drawn in little:** (1) made into a miniature painting; (2) brought together into the small space (of Malvolio's body); **Legion:** the name of the "unclean spirit" possessing the demoniac in Mark 5.9, whose response to Jesus was "My name is Legion; for we are many."

97. **private:** i.e., privacy

107. **an:** if

108. **at heart:** i.e., to heart

110. **water:** urine (for medical diagnosis); **wisewoman:** a woman who used charms or herbs to treat diseases

111. **Marry:** a mild oath, meaning "truly" or "indeed"

117. **move:** excite

117–18. **Let . . . him:** i.e., don't interfere

degree, but "fellow." Why, everything adheres together, that no dram of a scruple, no scruple of a scruple, no obstacle, no incredulous or unsafe circumstance—what can be said? Nothing that can be can come between me and the full prospect of my hopes. Well, Jove, not I, is the doer of this, and he is to be thanked.

Enter Toby, Fabian, and Maria.

TOBY Which way is he, in the name of sanctity? If all the devils of hell be drawn in little, and Legion himself possessed him, yet I'll speak to him.

FABIAN Here he is, here he is.—How is 't with you, sir? How is 't with you, man?

MALVOLIO Go off, I discard you. Let me enjoy my private. Go off.

MARIA, ⌜*to Toby*⌝ Lo, how hollow the fiend speaks within him! Did not I tell you? Sir Toby, my lady prays you to have a care of him.

MALVOLIO Aha, does she so?

TOBY, ⌜*to Fabian and Maria*⌝ Go to, go to! Peace, peace. We must deal gently with him. Let me alone.—How do you, Malvolio? How is 't with you? What, man, defy the devil! Consider, he's an enemy to mankind.

MALVOLIO Do you know what you say?

MARIA, ⌜*to Toby*⌝ La you, an you speak ill of the devil, how he takes it at heart! Pray God he be not bewitched!

FABIAN Carry his water to th' wisewoman.

MARIA Marry, and it shall be done tomorrow morning if I live. My lady would not lose him for more than I'll say.

MALVOLIO How now, mistress?

MARIA O Lord!

TOBY Prithee, hold thy peace. This is not the way. Do you not see you move him? Let me alone with him.

120. **rough:** violent; **used:** treated

121. **bawcock:** fine bird (French: *beau coq*) This word, along with **chuck** and **biddy** (both of which mean "chicken"), seems to be addressed to "the fiend" supposedly possessing Malvolio.

125. **for gravity:** i.e., appropriate for a dignified person; **cherry-pit:** a children's game

126. **foul collier:** dirty coal-dealer (applicable to Satan, who is pictured as black)

132. **idle:** frivolous

138. **genius:** i.e., soul

139. **device:** plot

140–41. **take . . . taint:** be exposed to the air (i.e., become known) and thus be ruined

144–45. **in . . . bound:** a standard treatment for insanity at the time

146. **carry it thus:** proceed in this way

149. **bar:** perhaps, the bar of justice, the open court

151. **matter . . . morning:** perhaps, sport fit for a holiday

FABIAN No way but gentleness, gently, gently. The fiend is rough and will not be roughly used.

TOBY, ⌜*to Malvolio*⌝ Why, how now, my bawcock? How dost thou, chuck?

MALVOLIO Sir!

TOBY Ay, biddy, come with me.—What, man, 'tis not for gravity to play at cherry-pit with Satan. Hang him, foul collier!

MARIA Get him to say his prayers, good Sir Toby; get him to pray.

MALVOLIO My prayers, minx?

MARIA, ⌜*to Toby*⌝ No, I warrant you, he will not hear of godliness.

MALVOLIO Go hang yourselves all! You are idle, shallow things. I am not of your element. You shall know more hereafter. *He exits.*

TOBY Is 't possible?

FABIAN If this were played upon a stage now, I could condemn it as an improbable fiction.

TOBY His very genius hath taken the infection of the device, man.

MARIA Nay, pursue him now, lest the device take air and taint.

FABIAN Why, we shall make him mad indeed.

MARIA The house will be the quieter.

TOBY Come, we'll have him in a dark room and bound. My niece is already in the belief that he's mad. We may carry it thus, for our pleasure and his penance, till our very pastime, tired out of breath, prompt us to have mercy on him, at which time we will bring the device to the bar and crown thee for a finder of madmen. But see, but see!

Enter Sir Andrew.

FABIAN More matter for a May morning.

ANDREW, ⌜*presenting a paper*⌝ Here's the challenge. Read it. I warrant there's vinegar and pepper in 't.

154. **saucy:** (1) flavored with seasoning; (2) insolent, rude

155. **warrant him:** perhaps, I can assure him (Cesario)

159. **admire:** marvel

162–63. **keeps . . . law:** i.e., protects you from arrest (for disturbing the peace, or for libel)

165. **thou liest in thy throat:** i.e., you are a complete liar

172. **o' th' windy side:** on the windward side, and therefore safe from attack

176. **look to:** i.e., look out for, take care of

179. **move him:** prompt him to action; or, arouse his feelings

182. **in some commerce:** in conversation about something

182–83. **by and by:** soon

184. **Scout me:** i.e., keep a lookout

185. **bum-baily:** a bailiff (sheriff's officer)

186. **draw:** i.e., draw your sword

189. **approbation:** reputation (for courage); **proof:** testing, trial

FABIAN Is 't so saucy?
ANDREW Ay, is 't. I warrant him. Do but read.
TOBY Give me. ⌈*He reads.*⌉ *Youth, whatsoever thou art, thou art but a scurvy fellow.*
FABIAN Good, and valiant.
TOBY ⌈*reads*⌉ *Wonder not, nor admire not in thy mind, why I do call thee so, for I will show thee no reason for 't.*
FABIAN A good note, that keeps you from the blow of the law.
TOBY ⌈*reads*⌉ *Thou com'st to the Lady Olivia, and in my sight she uses thee kindly. But thou liest in thy throat; that is not the matter I challenge thee for.*
FABIAN Very brief, and to exceeding good sense—less.
TOBY ⌈*reads*⌉ *I will waylay thee going home, where if it be thy chance to kill me—*
FABIAN Good.
TOBY ⌈*reads*⌉ *Thou kill'st me like a rogue and a villain.*
FABIAN Still you keep o' th' windy side of the law. Good.
TOBY ⌈*reads*⌉ *Fare thee well, and God have mercy upon one of our souls. He may have mercy upon mine, but my hope is better, and so look to thyself. Thy friend, as thou usest him, and thy sworn enemy,*
                                Andrew Aguecheek.
If this letter move him not, his legs cannot. I'll give 't him.
MARIA You may have very fit occasion for 't. He is now in some commerce with my lady, and will by and by depart.
TOBY Go, Sir Andrew. Scout me for him at the corner of the orchard like a bum-baily. So soon as ever thou seest him, draw, and as thou draw'st, swear horrible, for it comes to pass oft that a terrible oath, with a swaggering accent sharply twanged off, gives manhood more approbation than ever proof itself would have earned him. Away!

191. **let . . . swearing:** i.e., don't worry about my ability to swear

193. **gives him out:** shows him

194. **capacity:** intelligence; **breeding:** education; or, parentage; **his employment:** i.e., the service he performs

198. **clodpoll:** blockhead

199–200. **set . . . valor:** i.e., describe Aguecheek as notably courageous

204. **cockatrices:** mythical serpents (with the head, wings, and feet of a cock) whose looks could kill (See page 128.)

205–6. **Give them way:** i.e., let them alone

206. **presently after him:** immediately go after him

207. **horrid:** terrifying

210. **laid:** wagered; **unchary:** impetuously; **on 't:** perhaps, on that stony heart (Many editors change "on 't" to "out," and interpret the phrase as meaning "expended my honor too lavishly.")

214. **With . . . 'havior:** i.e., in the same way

215. **Goes on:** i.e., go on, persist

216. **jewel:** i.e., jeweled miniature portrait

220. **saved:** i.e., uncompromised

ANDREW Nay, let me alone for swearing. *He exits.*
TOBY Now will not I deliver his letter, for the behavior of the young gentleman gives him out to be of good capacity and breeding; his employment between his lord and my niece confirms no less. Therefore, this letter, being so excellently ignorant, will breed no terror in the youth. He will find it comes from a clodpoll. But, sir, I will deliver his challenge by word of mouth, set upon Aguecheek a notable report of valor, and drive the gentleman (as I know his youth will aptly receive it) into a most hideous opinion of his rage, skill, fury, and impetuosity. This will so fright them both that they will kill one another by the look, like cockatrices.

Enter Olivia and Viola.

FABIAN Here he comes with your niece. Give them way till he take leave, and presently after him.
TOBY I will meditate the while upon some horrid message for a challenge.
⌜*Toby, Fabian, and Maria exit.*⌝

OLIVIA
I have said too much unto a heart of stone
And laid mine honor too unchary on 't.
There's something in me that reproves my fault,
But such a headstrong potent fault it is
That it but mocks reproof.

VIOLA
With the same 'havior that your passion bears
Goes on my master's griefs.

OLIVIA
Here, wear this jewel for me. 'Tis my picture.
Refuse it not. It hath no tongue to vex you.
And I beseech you come again tomorrow.
What shall you ask of me that I'll deny,
That honor, saved, may upon asking give?

229. **defense:** ability as a fencer; **betake thee:** commit yourself (Sir Toby speaks to Cesario in very contorted language throughout this scene.)

231. **thy intercepter:** i.e., the one who wants to cut you off; **despite:** anger, defiance

232. **hunter:** perhaps, huntsman; or, perhaps, hunting dog; **attends thee:** waits for you

232–33. **Dismount thy tuck:** draw your sword

233. **yare:** quick

236. **to:** i.e., with; **remembrance:** memory; **free:** innocent

239. **price:** value

239–40. **betake . . . guard:** put yourself in a defensive position (See page 130.)

240. **opposite:** adversary

241. **withal:** i.e., with

243. **dubbed:** made a knight; **unhatched:** unhacked, not used (This charge, and the admission that Sir Andrew's knighthood was for **carpet consideration**—i.e., that he was knighted at court rather than on the battlefield—acknowledge that he is no soldier.)

246. **incensement:** anger

247. **satisfaction . . . by:** i.e., he can be satisfied only by

248–49. **"Hob, nob," "give 't or take 't":** Both phrases mean that the challenger wants to fight to the death. **word:** motto

124

VIOLA
Nothing but this: your true love for my master.
OLIVIA
How with mine honor may I give him that
Which I have given to you?
VIOLA   I will acquit you.
OLIVIA
Well, come again tomorrow. Fare thee well.   225
A fiend like thee might bear my soul to hell.
⌜*She exits.*⌝

Enter Toby and Fabian.

TOBY Gentleman, God save thee.
VIOLA And you, sir.
TOBY That defense thou hast, betake thee to 't. Of what nature the wrongs are thou hast done him, I know not, but thy intercepter, full of despite, bloody as the hunter, attends thee at the orchard end. Dismount thy tuck, be yare in thy preparation, for thy assailant is quick, skillful, and deadly.   230
VIOLA You mistake, sir. I am sure no man hath any quarrel to me. My remembrance is very free and clear from any image of offense done to any man.   235
TOBY You'll find it otherwise, I assure you. Therefore, if you hold your life at any price, betake you to your guard, for your opposite hath in him what youth, strength, skill, and wrath can furnish man withal.   240
VIOLA I pray you, sir, what is he?
TOBY He is knight dubbed with unhatched rapier and on carpet consideration, but he is a devil in private brawl. Souls and bodies hath he divorced three, and his incensement at this moment is so implacable that satisfaction can be none but by pangs of death and sepulcher. "Hob, nob" is his word; "give 't or take 't."   245
VIOLA I will return again into the house and desire   250

251. **conduct:** escort; **of:** from
252–53. **put quarrels . . . on:** i.e., provoke quarrels with
253. **taste:** test; **Belike:** perhaps
255. **derives itself:** i.e., grows
256. **competent injury:** i.e., an insult sufficient to demand satisfaction
258. **that:** i.e., a duel
259. **answer:** fight with
260. **meddle:** fight
261–62. **forswear . . . you:** i.e., give up your right to wear a sword (admit your cowardice)
263. **uncivil:** rude
264. **office:** kindness, service; **as . . . of:** i.e., find out from
266. **negligence:** oversight; **purpose:** intention
271. **a . . . arbitrament:** i.e., a fight to the death
274. **read:** judge
275. **form:** appearance; **like:** likely

some conduct of the lady. I am no fighter. I have heard of some kind of men that put quarrels purposely on others to taste their valor. Belike this is a man of that quirk.

TOBY Sir, no. His indignation derives itself out of a very competent injury. Therefore get you on and give him his desire. Back you shall not to the house, unless you undertake that with me which with as much safety you might answer him. Therefore on, or strip your sword stark naked, for meddle you must, that's certain, or forswear to wear iron about you.

VIOLA This is as uncivil as strange. I beseech you, do me this courteous office, as to know of the knight what my offense to him is. It is something of my negligence, nothing of my purpose.

TOBY I will do so.—Signior Fabian, stay you by this gentleman till my return. *Toby exits.*

VIOLA Pray you, sir, do you know of this matter?

FABIAN I know the knight is incensed against you even to a mortal arbitrament, but nothing of the circumstance more.

VIOLA I beseech you, what manner of man is he?

FABIAN Nothing of that wonderful promise, to read him by his form, as you are like to find him in the proof of his valor. He is indeed, sir, the most skillful, bloody, and fatal opposite that you could possibly have found in any part of Illyria. Will you walk towards him? I will make your peace with him if I can.

VIOLA I shall be much bound to you for 't. I am one that had rather go with Sir Priest than Sir Knight, I care not who knows so much of my mettle.
They exit.

Enter Toby and Andrew.

285. **firago:** virago; **pass:** bout
286. **stuck-in:** stoccata (a fencing thrust)
288. **answer:** return thrust
290. **Sophy:** shah of Persia
291. **Pox on 't:** a mild oath
295. **fence:** i.e., fencing
299. **motion:** offer
300. **on 't:** of it
303. **take up:** settle
305. **He:** Cesario; **is . . . conceited:** has as horrible an image
310. **his quarrel:** i.e., the insult to him
311–12. **for . . . vow:** so that he can keep his oath

A cockatrice. (3.4.204)
From Joachim Camerarius, *Symbolorum et emblematum* (1605).

TOBY Why, man, he's a very devil. I have not seen such a firago. I had a pass with him, rapier, scabbard, and all, and he gives me the stuck-in with such a mortal motion that it is inevitable; and on the answer, he pays you as surely as your feet hits the ground they step on. They say he has been fencer to the Sophy.

ANDREW Pox on 't! I'll not meddle with him.

TOBY Ay, but he will not now be pacified. Fabian can scarce hold him yonder.

ANDREW Plague on 't! An I thought he had been valiant and so cunning in fence, I'd have seen him damned ere I'd have challenged him. Let him let the matter slip, and I'll give him my horse, gray Capilet.

TOBY I'll make the motion. Stand here, make a good show on 't. This shall end without the perdition of souls. ⌜*Aside.*⌝ Marry, I'll ride your horse as well as I ride you.

Enter Fabian and Viola.

⌜*Toby crosses to meet them.*⌝
⌜*Aside to Fabian.*⌝ I have his horse to take up the quarrel. I have persuaded him the youth's a devil.

FABIAN, ⌜*aside to Toby*⌝ He is as horribly conceited of him, and pants and looks pale as if a bear were at his heels.

TOBY, ⌜*to Viola*⌝ There's no remedy, sir; he will fight with you for 's oath sake. Marry, he hath better bethought him of his quarrel, and he finds that now scarce to be worth talking of. Therefore, draw for the supportance of his vow. He protests he will not hurt you.

VIOLA Pray God defend me! ⌜*Aside.*⌝ A little thing would make me tell them how much I lack of a man.

320. **duello:** dueling code
332. **undertaker:** i.e., one who undertakes to fight
334. **anon:** soon
337. **for that:** as for that which (i.e., my horse)

"Betake you to your guard." (3.4.239–40)
From George Silver, *Paradoxes of defence* (1599).

FABIAN Give ground if you see him furious.
⌜*Toby crosses to Andrew.*⌝
TOBY Come, Sir Andrew, there's no remedy. The gentleman will, for his honor's sake, have one bout with you. He cannot by the *duello* avoid it. But he has promised me, as he is a gentleman and a soldier, he will not hurt you. Come on, to 't.
ANDREW, ⌜*drawing his sword*⌝ Pray God he keep his oath!
VIOLA, ⌜*drawing her sword*⌝
I do assure you, 'tis against my will.

Enter Antonio.

ANTONIO, ⌜*to Andrew*⌝
Put up your sword. If this young gentleman
Have done offense, I take the fault on me.
If you offend him, I for him defy you.
TOBY You, sir? Why, what are you?
ANTONIO, ⌜*drawing his sword*⌝
One, sir, that for his love dares yet do more
Than you have heard him brag to you he will.
TOBY, ⌜*drawing his sword*⌝
Nay, if you be an undertaker, I am for you.

Enter Officers.

FABIAN O, good Sir Toby, hold! Here come the officers.
TOBY, ⌜*to Antonio*⌝ I'll be with you anon.
VIOLA, ⌜*to Andrew*⌝ Pray, sir, put your sword up, if you please.
ANDREW Marry, will I, sir. And for that I promised you, I'll be as good as my word. He will bear you easily, and reins well.
FIRST OFFICER This is the man. Do thy office.
SECOND OFFICER Antonio, I arrest thee at the suit of Count Orsino.
ANTONIO You do mistake me, sir.

344. **favor:** face
353. **amazed:** bewildered, perplexed
359. **part:** i.e., partly
361. **My having:** i.e., the money that I have
362. **present:** i.e., my present funds
365. **deserts:** good deeds, services
366. **lack persuasion:** i.e., fail to persuade (you to help me)
367. **unsound:** wicked
373. **vainness:** (1) vanity; (2) foolishness
375. **blood:** nature

FIRST OFFICER
No, sir, no jot. I know your favor well,
Though now you have no sea-cap on your head.— 345
Take him away. He knows I know him well.
ANTONIO
I must obey. ⌜*To Viola.*⌝ This comes with seeking you.
But there's no remedy. I shall answer it.
What will you do, now my necessity 350
Makes me to ask you for my purse? It grieves me
Much more for what I cannot do for you
Than what befalls myself. You stand amazed,
But be of comfort.
SECOND OFFICER   Come, sir, away. 355
ANTONIO, ⌜*to Viola*⌝
I must entreat of you some of that money.
VIOLA What money, sir?
For the fair kindness you have showed me here,
And part being prompted by your present trouble,
Out of my lean and low ability 360
I'll lend you something. My having is not much.
I'll make division of my present with you.
Hold, there's half my coffer.   ⌜*Offering him money.*⌝
ANTONIO Will you deny me now?
Is 't possible that my deserts to you 365
Can lack persuasion? Do not tempt my misery,
Lest that it make me so unsound a man
As to upbraid you with those kindnesses
That I have done for you.
VIOLA   I know of none, 370
Nor know I you by voice or any feature.
I hate ingratitude more in a man
Than lying, vainness, babbling drunkenness,
Or any taint of vice whose strong corruption
Inhabits our frail blood— 375
ANTONIO   O heavens themselves!

379. **one half ... death:** i.e., half-dead

385. **done ... shame:** i.e., disgraced your good looks

386. **the mind:** i.e., what happens in one's mind or heart

389. **empty ... devil:** i.e., elaborately decorated chests, made beautiful by the devil but with nothing inside

393. **passion:** intense feelings

398. **saws:** sayings

400. **glass:** mirror

401. **favor:** looks, features

402. **Still:** always

Luna. (1.5.198)
From Johann Engel, *Astrolabium* (1488).

SECOND OFFICER Come, sir, I pray you go.
ANTONIO
  Let me speak a little. This youth that you see here
  I snatched one half out of the jaws of death,
  Relieved him with such sanctity of love,   380
  And to his image, which methought did promise
  Most venerable worth, did I devotion.
FIRST OFFICER
  What's that to us? The time goes by. Away!
ANTONIO
  But O, how vile an idol proves this god!
  Thou hast, Sebastian, done good feature shame.   385
  In nature there's no blemish but the mind;
  None can be called deformed but the unkind.
  Virtue is beauty, but the beauteous evil
  Are empty trunks o'erflourished by the devil.
FIRST OFFICER
  The man grows mad. Away with him.—Come,   390
    come, sir.
ANTONIO Lead me on.
             ⌜*Antonio and Officers* exit.⌝
VIOLA, ⌜*aside*⌝
  Methinks his words do from such passion fly
  That he believes himself; so do not I.
  Prove true, imagination, O, prove true,   395
  That I, dear brother, be now ta'en for you!
TOBY Come hither, knight; come hither, Fabian. We'll
    whisper o'er a couplet or two of most sage saws.
             ⌜*Toby, Fabian, and Andrew move aside.*⌝
VIOLA
  He named Sebastian. I my brother know
  Yet living in my glass. Even such and so   400
  In favor was my brother, and he went
  Still in this fashion, color, ornament,
  For him I imitate. O, if it prove,
  Tempests are kind, and salt waves fresh in love!
                              ⌜*She exits.*⌝

405. **dishonest:** dishonorable, shameful
409–10. **religious in:** i.e., devoted to
411. **'Slid:** an oath "by God's eyelid"
415. **event:** outcome

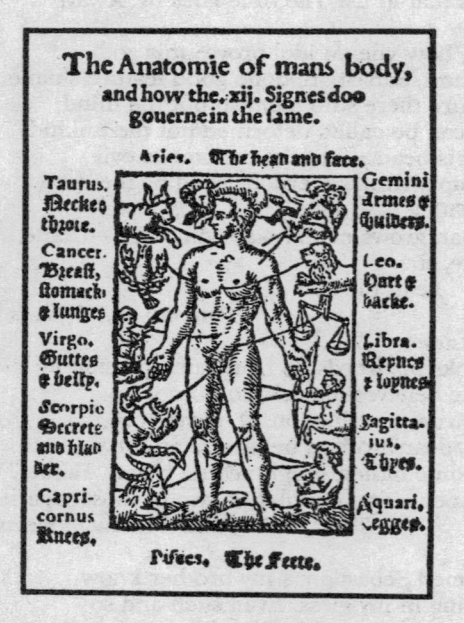

The Anatomie of mans body,
and how the .xij. Signes doo gouerne in the same.

Aries. The head and face.

Taurus. Necke & throte.

Gemini Armes & shulders.

Cancer. Breast, stomack & lunges

Leo. Hart & backe.

Virgo. Guttes & belly.

Libra. Reynes & loynes.

Scorpio. Secretes and bladder.

Sagittarius. Thyes.

Capricornus Knees.

Aquarius. Legges.

Pisces. The Feete.

The signs governing the body. (1.3.135)
From Walter Gray, *An almanacke* ... (1591).

TOBY A very dishonest, paltry boy, and more a coward than a hare. His dishonesty appears in leaving his friend here in necessity and denying him; and for his cowardship, ask Fabian.

FABIAN A coward, a most devout coward, religious in it.

ANDREW 'Slid, I'll after him again and beat him.

TOBY Do, cuff him soundly, but never draw thy sword.

ANDREW An I do not—

FABIAN Come, let's see the event.

TOBY I dare lay any money 'twill be nothing yet.
⌜*They*⌝ *exit.*

TWELFTH NIGHT, OR, WHAT YOU WILL

ACT 4

4.1 The Fool encounters Sebastian, whom he mistakes for Cesario. When Sir Andrew and Sir Toby attack Sebastian, the Fool fetches Olivia, who again declares her love—this time to a delighted Sebastian.

---

3. **Go to:** an expression of impatience
5. **held out:** kept up, maintained
5–9. **I . . . so:** These lines are said sarcastically.
10. **vent:** give expression to
14. **lubber:** oaf
15. **cockney:** sissy; **ungird:** remove
15–16. **strangeness:** distance (i.e., pretense that you and I are strangers)
18. **foolish Greek:** A "merry Greek" was a buffoon or jester.

A Fool.
From August Redel, *Apophtegmata* . . . (n.d.).

ACT 4

Scene 1
Enter Sebastian and ⌜Feste, the Fool.⌝

FOOL Will you make me believe that I am not sent for you?

SEBASTIAN Go to, go to, thou art a foolish fellow. Let me be clear of thee.

FOOL Well held out, i' faith. No, I do not know you, nor I am not sent to you by my lady to bid you come speak with her, nor your name is not Master Cesario, nor this is not my nose neither. Nothing that is so is so.

SEBASTIAN I prithee, vent thy folly somewhere else. Thou know'st not me.

FOOL Vent my folly? He has heard that word of some great man and now applies it to a Fool. Vent my folly? I am afraid this great lubber the world will prove a cockney. I prithee now, ungird thy strangeness and tell me what I shall vent to my lady. Shall I vent to her that thou art coming?

SEBASTIAN I prithee, foolish Greek, depart from me. There's money for thee. ⌜*Giving money.*⌝ If you tarry longer, I shall give worse payment.

FOOL By my troth, thou hast an open hand. These wise men that give Fools money get themselves a good report—after fourteen years' purchase.

28. **your dagger:** These words have suggested to some editors that Sebastian beats Andrew with the hilt of his dagger. If such is the case, Toby's command to Sebastian at line 39, "put up your iron," would mean "sheathe your dagger."

30. **straight:** straightway, immediately

34. **action of battery:** i.e., lawsuit accusing him of unlawfully beating me

39. **fleshed:** eager for battle; or, hardened to battle

45. **malapert:** impudent

Fortune. (2.4.92)
From George Wither, *A collection of emblemes* . . . (1635).

Enter Andrew, Toby, and Fabian.

ANDREW, ⌜*to Sebastian*⌝ Now, sir, have I met you again?
There's for you.   ⌜*He strikes Sebastian.*⌝

SEBASTIAN, ⌜*returning the blow*⌝ Why, there's for thee,
and there, and there.—Are all the people mad?

TOBY Hold, sir, or I'll throw your dagger o'er the
house.

FOOL, ⌜*aside*⌝ This will I tell my lady straight. I would
not be in some of your coats for twopence.
⌜*He exits.*⌝

TOBY, ⌜*seizing Sebastian*⌝ Come on, sir, hold!

ANDREW Nay, let him alone. I'll go another way to
work with him. I'll have an action of battery against
him, if there be any law in Illyria. Though I struck
him first, yet it's no matter for that.

SEBASTIAN, ⌜*to Toby*⌝ Let go thy hand!

TOBY Come, sir, I will not let you go. Come, my young
soldier, put up your iron. You are well fleshed.
Come on.

SEBASTIAN
I will be free from thee.
⌜*He pulls free and draws his sword.*⌝
                    What wouldst thou now?
If thou dar'st tempt me further, draw thy sword.

TOBY What, what? Nay, then, I must have an ounce or
two of this malapert blood from you.
⌜*He draws his sword.*⌝

Enter Olivia.

OLIVIA
Hold, Toby! On thy life I charge thee, hold!

TOBY Madam.

OLIVIA
Will it be ever thus? Ungracious wretch,
Fit for the mountains and the barbarous caves,

53. **Rudesby:** ruffian
56. **extent:** assault
59. **botched up:** clumsily put together
61. **deny:** refuse; **Beshrew:** literally, curse (but the harshness of the word was lost through repeated use)
62. **started . . . thee:** i.e., made my heart (residing in you) leap with fear (There is a play on **heart** and "hart" and on **start** as "startle" and "rouse an animal from its hiding place.")
63. **What . . . this:** i.e., what does this mean? (literally, how does this taste?)
64. **Or . . . or:** either . . . or
65. **Let . . . steep:** i.e., let me continue in this dreamlike state **fancy:** imagination **sense:** senses, awareness of the waking world **Lethe:** the mythological river in the underworld that washes away one's memory of one's former life **steep:** immerse
67. **Would:** i.e., I wish

4.2 Under directions from Sir Toby, the Fool disguises himself as a parish priest and visits the imprisoned Malvolio. In his own person, the Fool agrees to fetch pen, paper, and a candle for the supposed madman.

---

2. **curate:** parish priest
3. **the whilst:** i.e., in the meantime
4. **dissemble:** disguise
5. **dissembled:** played the hypocrite

Where manners ne'er were preached! Out of my sight!— 50
Be not offended, dear Cesario.—
Rudesby, begone! ⌜*Toby, Andrew, and Fabian exit.*⌝
                    I prithee, gentle friend,
Let thy fair wisdom, not thy passion, sway 55
In this uncivil and unjust extent
Against thy peace. Go with me to my house,
And hear thou there how many fruitless pranks
This ruffian hath botched up, that thou thereby
Mayst smile at this. Thou shalt not choose but go. 60
Do not deny. Beshrew his soul for me!
He started one poor heart of mine, in thee.

SEBASTIAN, ⌜*aside*⌝
What relish is in this? How runs the stream?
Or I am mad, or else this is a dream.
Let fancy still my sense in Lethe steep; 65
If it be thus to dream, still let me sleep!

OLIVIA
Nay, come, I prithee. Would thou'dst be ruled by me!

SEBASTIAN
Madam, I will.

OLIVIA   O, say so, and so be! 70
                                 They exit.

Scene 2
Enter Maria and ⌜Feste, the Fool.⌝

MARIA Nay, I prithee, put on this gown and this beard; make him believe thou art Sir Topas the curate. Do it quickly. I'll call Sir Toby the whilst. ⌜*She exits.*⌝

FOOL Well, I'll put it on, and I will dissemble myself in 't, and I would I were the first that ever dissembled in such a gown. ⌜*He puts on gown and beard.*⌝ I am 5

7. **the function:** i.e., of a priest
9. **housekeeper:** hospitable person
11. **The competitors:** i.e., my colleagues
13. **Bonos dies:** good day (in bad Latin)
13–14. **the ... Prague:** The Fool once again invents an authority to quote in his foolery.
15. **Gorboduc:** a legendary king of Britain
18. **To him:** i.e., begin your attack on Malvolio
21 SD. **Malvolio within:** This Folio direction indicates that Malvolio speaks from offstage or from behind a door or curtain.
27. **Out ... fiend:** addressed to the devil that supposedly possesses Malvolio **hyperbolical:** i.e., ranting (literally, using hyperbole or exaggeration)
33. **dishonest:** dishonorable; lying
34. **modest:** moderate

not tall enough to become the function well, nor lean enough to be thought a good student, but to be said an honest man and a good housekeeper goes as fairly as to say a careful man and a great scholar. The competitors enter.

Enter Toby ⌈and Maria.⌉

TOBY Jove bless thee, Master Parson.
FOOL *Bonos dies*, Sir Toby; for, as the old hermit of Prague, that never saw pen and ink, very wittily said to a niece of King Gorboduc "That that is, is," so I, being Master Parson, am Master Parson; for what is "that" but "that" and "is" but "is"?
TOBY To him, Sir Topas.
FOOL, ⌈*disguising his voice*⌉ What ho, I say! Peace in this prison!
TOBY The knave counterfeits well. A good knave.

Malvolio within.

MALVOLIO Who calls there?
FOOL Sir Topas the curate, who comes to visit Malvolio the lunatic.
MALVOLIO Sir Topas, Sir Topas, good Sir Topas, go to my lady—
FOOL Out, hyperbolical fiend! How vexest thou this man! Talkest thou nothing but of ladies?
TOBY, ⌈*aside*⌉ Well said, Master Parson.
MALVOLIO Sir Topas, never was man thus wronged. Good Sir Topas, do not think I am mad. They have laid me here in hideous darkness—
FOOL Fie, thou dishonest Satan! I call thee by the most modest terms, for I am one of those gentle ones that will use the devil himself with courtesy. Sayst thou that house is dark?
MALVOLIO As hell, Sir Topas.

38–39. **barricadoes:** barricades, barriers

39. **clerestories:** high windows

45. **puzzled:** confused

46. **the . . . fog:** In stories about Moses, one of the plagues visited by God on the Egyptians was "a thick darkness in all the land of Egypt three days" (Exodus 10.22).

50–51. **any constant question:** perhaps, any consistent line of questioning

52. **Pythagoras:** This ancient Greek philosopher taught the transmigration of souls. Ovid's *Metamorphoses* (a book used frequently by Shakespeare) has a speech by Pythagoras urging humans not to kill animals because "Our souls survive . . . death; as they depart / Their local habitations in the flesh, / They enter new-found bodies that preserve them. / . . . the spirit takes its way / To different kinds of being as it chooses, / From beast to man, from man to beast." (Book 15, trans. Horace Gregory)

54. **haply:** perhaps

61. **allow . . . wits:** agree that you're sane; **and fear:** and (until) you shall fear

66. **I . . . waters:** perhaps, I can do anything

71–72. **delivered:** freed

FOOL Why, it hath bay windows transparent as barricadoes, and the ⌈clerestories⌉ toward the south-north are as lustrous as ebony; and yet complainest thou of obstruction?

MALVOLIO I am not mad, Sir Topas. I say to you this house is dark.

FOOL Madman, thou errest. I say there is no darkness but ignorance, in which thou art more puzzled than the Egyptians in their fog.

MALVOLIO I say this house is as dark as ignorance, though ignorance were as dark as hell. And I say there was never man thus abused. I am no more mad than you are. Make the trial of it in any constant question.

FOOL What is the opinion of Pythagoras concerning wildfowl?

MALVOLIO That the soul of our grandam might haply inhabit a bird.

FOOL What thinkst thou of his opinion?

MALVOLIO I think nobly of the soul, and no way approve his opinion.

FOOL Fare thee well. Remain thou still in darkness. Thou shalt hold th' opinion of Pythagoras ere I will allow of thy wits, and fear to kill a woodcock lest thou dispossess the soul of thy grandam. Fare thee well.

MALVOLIO Sir Topas, Sir Topas!

TOBY My most exquisite Sir Topas!

FOOL Nay, I am for all waters.

MARIA Thou mightst have done this without thy beard and gown. He sees thee not.

TOBY To him in thine own voice, and bring me word how thou find'st him. I would we were well rid of this knavery. If he may be conveniently delivered, I would he were, for I am now so far in offense with my niece that I cannot pursue with

74. **the upshot:** i.e., to its final conclusion
76. **Hey, Robin . . . :** a song the words for which are attributed to Thomas Wyatt
79. **perdy:** for sure (*par Dieu*, by God)
91. **fell you besides:** i.e., did you lose; **five wits:** five senses; or, according to Stephen Hawes in *The Pastime of Pleasure*, the five wits are common wit, imagination, fantasy, estimation, and memory
94. **But:** i.e., only, no more than
96. **propertied me:** treated me like a lifeless object
98. **face:** bully
99. **Advise you:** i.e., be careful

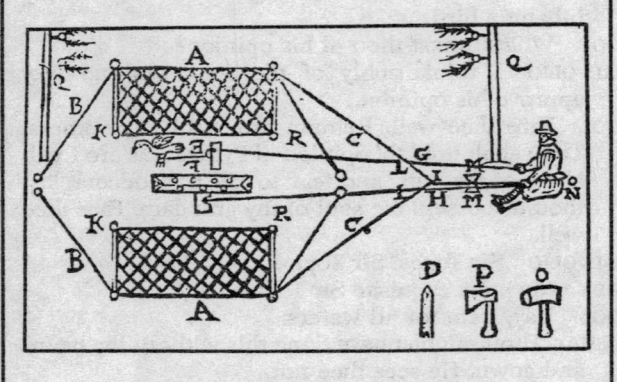

A woodcock in a "gin." (2.5.85)
From Gervase Markham, *Hunger's prevention, or, The whole art of fowling . . .* (1655).

any safety this sport the upshot. Come by and by
to my chamber.

⌜Toby and Maria⌝ exit.

FOOL ⌜*sings, in his own voice*⌝
> *Hey, Robin, jolly Robin,*
> *Tell me how thy lady does.*

MALVOLIO Fool!

FOOL ⌜*sings*⌝
> *My lady is unkind, perdy.*

MALVOLIO Fool!

FOOL ⌜*sings*⌝
> *Alas, why is she so?*

MALVOLIO Fool, I say!

FOOL ⌜*sings*⌝
> *She loves another—*

Who calls, ha?

MALVOLIO Good Fool, as ever thou wilt deserve well at my hand, help me to a candle, and pen, ink, and paper. As I am a gentleman, I will live to be thankful to thee for 't.

FOOL Master Malvolio?

MALVOLIO Ay, good Fool.

FOOL Alas, sir, how fell you besides your five wits?

MALVOLIO Fool, there was never man so notoriously abused. I am as well in my wits, Fool, as thou art.

FOOL But as well? Then you are mad indeed, if you be no better in your wits than a Fool.

MALVOLIO They have here propertied me, keep me in darkness, send ministers to me—asses!—and do all they can to face me out of my wits.

FOOL Advise you what you say. The minister is here. ⌜*In the voice of Sir Topas.*⌝ Malvolio, Malvolio, thy wits the heavens restore. Endeavor thyself to sleep and leave thy vain bibble-babble.

MALVOLIO Sir Topas!

105–6. **God buy you:** i.e., God be with you, goodbye

110. **shent:** rebuked

114. **Welladay that:** i.e., alas, if only

117. **advantage:** benefit, profit

118. **letter:** i.e., a letter

128. **the old Vice:** a comic character in earlier drama, whose props (dagger of **lath,** or wood) and antics are described in the lines of the song

133. **goodman:** a title indicating a low social rank

"Shall we make the welkin dance?" (2.3.58)
From *Image du monde. The myrrour-dyscrypcyon of the worled . . .* (1527).

FOOL, ⌜*as Sir Topas*⌝ Maintain no words with him, good
fellow. ⌜*As Fool.*⌝ Who, I, sir? Not I, sir! God buy
you, good Sir Topas. ⌜*As Sir Topas.*⌝ Marry, amen.
⌜*As Fool.*⌝ I will, sir, I will.
MALVOLIO Fool! Fool! Fool, I say!
FOOL Alas, sir, be patient. What say you, sir? I am
shent for speaking to you.
MALVOLIO Good Fool, help me to some light and some
paper. I tell thee, I am as well in my wits as any
man in Illyria.
FOOL Welladay that you were, sir!
MALVOLIO By this hand, I am. Good Fool, some ink,
paper, and light; and convey what I will set down to
my lady. It shall advantage thee more than ever the
bearing of letter did.
FOOL I will help you to 't. But tell me true, are you not
mad indeed, or do you but counterfeit?
MALVOLIO Believe me, I am not. I tell thee true.
FOOL Nay, I'll ne'er believe a madman till I see his
brains. I will fetch you light and paper and ink.
MALVOLIO Fool, I'll requite it in the highest degree. I
prithee, begone.
FOOL ⌜*sings*⌝
I am gone, sir, and anon, sir,
  I'll be with you again,
In a trice, like to the old Vice,
  Your need to sustain.
Who with dagger of lath, in his rage and his wrath,
  Cries "aha!" to the devil;
Like a mad lad, "Pare thy nails, dad!
  Adieu, goodman devil."

He exits.

4.3 While Sebastian is sure that neither he nor Olivia is insane, he is amazed by the wonder of his new situation. When Olivia asks him to enter into a formal betrothal with her, he readily agrees.

---

3. **wonder:** a state of mind caused by experiencing the wonderful or miraculous
6. **there he was:** i.e., he had been there; **credit:** report
7. **range:** roam, wander around
9. **my soul ... sense:** i.e., my reason and my senses agree in arguing
12. **instance:** example; **discourse:** reasoning
15. **trust:** belief
17. **sway:** rule
19. **Take ... dispatch:** i.e., "take affairs" (undertake business matters) and "give back their dispatch" (complete them promptly)
22. **deceivable:** deceptive
25. **chantry:** chapel; **by:** nearby
27. **Plight ... faith:** i.e., assure me of your fidelity (through a betrothal)
28. **jealous:** anxious; **doubtful:** filled with doubts, insecure
29. **He:** i.e., the priest

154

Scene 3
Enter Sebastian.

⌜SEBASTIAN⌝
This is the air; that is the glorious sun.
This pearl she gave me, I do feel 't and see 't.
And though 'tis wonder that enwraps me thus,
Yet 'tis not madness. Where's Antonio, then?
I could not find him at the Elephant. 5
Yet there he was; and there I found this credit,
That he did range the town to seek me out.
His counsel now might do me golden service.
For though my soul disputes well with my sense
That this may be some error, but no madness, 10
Yet doth this accident and flood of fortune
So far exceed all instance, all discourse,
That I am ready to distrust mine eyes
And wrangle with my reason that persuades me
To any other trust but that I am mad— 15
Or else the lady's mad. Yet if 'twere so,
She could not sway her house, command her
  followers,
Take and give back affairs and their dispatch
With such a smooth, discreet, and stable bearing 20
As I perceive she does. There's something in 't
That is deceivable. But here the lady comes.

Enter Olivia and ⌜a⌝ Priest.

OLIVIA, ⌜*to Sebastian*⌝
Blame not this haste of mine. If you mean well,
Now go with me and with this holy man
Into the chantry by. There, before him 25
And underneath that consecrated roof,
Plight me the full assurance of your faith,
That my most jealous and too doubtful soul
May live at peace. He shall conceal it

30. **Whiles:** until; **come to note:** become known
31. **What time:** at which time; **our ... keep:** i.e., celebrate our marriage
32. **birth:** social rank
37. **fairly note:** look favorably on; or, show that they approve

Dancing the galliard. (1.3.117)
From Fabritio Caroso, *Il ballarino* ... (1581).

Whiles you are willing it shall come to note, 30
What time we will our celebration keep
According to my birth. What do you say?

SEBASTIAN
I'll follow this good man and go with you
And, having sworn truth, ever will be true.

OLIVIA
Then lead the way, good father, and heavens so shine 35
That they may fairly note this act of mine.

They exit.

TWELFTH NIGHT,
OR,
WHAT YOU WILL

ACT 5

5.1 Orsino, at Olivia's estate, sends the Fool to bring Olivia to him. Antonio is brought in by officers and he tells the incredulous Orsino about Cesario's treacherous behavior. At Olivia's entrance, Orsino expresses his anger that Cesario has become Olivia's darling. Cesario's expressions of love for Orsino lead Olivia to send for the "holy father," who confirms Olivia's claim that she is formally betrothed to Cesario. Sir Andrew and Sir Toby enter with bloody heads, which they blame on Cesario. Sebastian's entry at this moment untangles a series of knots: Sebastian addresses Olivia with love, greets Antonio warmly, and recognizes Cesario as the image of himself. When Cesario admits to being Sebastian's sister Viola, Orsino asks Viola to become his wife. On the day that Sebastian marries Olivia, Viola will marry Orsino.

---

18. **abused:** deceived
18–20. **conclusions . . . affirmatives:** possibly an allusion to a sonnet by Sir Philip Sidney, in which the lady's twice saying "no" is taken as a "yes" because, in grammar, two negatives make an affirmative

ACT 5

Scene 1
Enter ⌜Feste, the Fool⌝ and Fabian.

FABIAN Now, as thou lov'st me, let me see his letter.
FOOL Good Master Fabian, grant me another request.
FABIAN Anything.
FOOL Do not desire to see this letter.
FABIAN This is to give a dog and in recompense desire my dog again.

Enter ⌜Orsino,⌝ Viola, Curio, and Lords.

ORSINO
Belong you to the Lady Olivia, friends?
FOOL Ay, sir, we are some of her trappings.
ORSINO
I know thee well. How dost thou, my good fellow?
FOOL Truly, sir, the better for my foes and the worse for my friends.
ORSINO
Just the contrary: the better for thy friends.
FOOL No, sir, the worse.
ORSINO How can that be?
FOOL Marry, sir, they praise me and make an ass of me. Now my foes tell me plainly I am an ass; so that by my foes, sir, I profit in the knowledge of myself, and by my friends I am abused. So that, conclusions to be as kisses, if your four negatives make your two

26. **double-dealing:** (1) giving twice; (2) duplicity

29. **grace:** virtue (with a pun on the phrase—"your Grace"—with which the duke is normally addressed)

30. **obey it:** i.e., obey the Fool's **ill counsel**

33. **Primo, secundo, tertio:** first, second, third (perhaps an allusion to a children's game, or **play**)

34. **triplex:** triple time in music (i.e., a three-beat rhythm)

35. **tripping:** quick and light

35. **Saint Bennet:** i.e., the church of St. Benedict

37. **fool:** beg through clever wordplay

38. **throw:** i.e., time (literally, throw of the dice)

43. **desire of having:** i.e., wish to possess

45. **anon:** very soon

49. **Vulcan:** Roman god of war and blacksmith to the gods

50. **baubling:** tiny, insignificant

Vulcan. (5.1.49)
From Johann Basilius Heroldt, *Heydenwelt* . . . (1554).

affirmatives, why then the worse for my friends and the better for my foes.

ORSINO Why, this is excellent.

FOOL By my troth, sir, no—though it please you to be one of my friends.

ORSINO, ⌜*giving a coin*⌝
Thou shalt not be the worse for me; there's gold.

FOOL But that it would be double-dealing, sir, I would you could make it another.

ORSINO O, you give me ill counsel.

FOOL Put your grace in your pocket, sir, for this once, and let your flesh and blood obey it.

ORSINO Well, I will be so much a sinner to be a double-dealer: there's another. ⌜*He gives a coin.*⌝

FOOL *Primo, secundo, tertio* is a good play, and the old saying is, the third pays for all. The triplex, sir, is a good tripping measure, or the bells of Saint Bennet, sir, may put you in mind—one, two, three.

ORSINO You can fool no more money out of me at this throw. If you will let your lady know I am here to speak with her, and bring her along with you, it may awake my bounty further.

FOOL Marry, sir, lullaby to your bounty till I come again. I go, sir, but I would not have you to think that my desire of having is the sin of covetousness. But, as you say, sir, let your bounty take a nap. I will awake it anon. *He exits.*

Enter Antonio and Officers.

VIOLA
Here comes the man, sir, that did rescue me.

ORSINO
That face of his I do remember well.
Yet when I saw it last, it was besmeared
As black as Vulcan in the smoke of war.
A baubling vessel was he captain of,

51. **For ... unprizable:** i.e., worthless because of its **shallow draught** and its small **bulk**

52. **With which:** i.e., with which worthless vessel; **scatheful:** harmful

53. **bottom:** ship

54. **very:** even; **tongue of loss:** i.e., voices of those whom he defeated

55. **Cried:** called out

57. **fraught:** freight, that which the ship carries; **Candy:** Candia (capital of Crete)

60. **desperate of:** i.e., as if unconcerned with; **state:** i.e., his situation

61. **brabble:** brawl

62. **drew ... side:** i.e., drew his sword to defend me

63. **put ... me:** talked to me strangely

64. **distraction:** madness

67. **dear:** dire

73. **base and ground:** evidence

77. **wrack:** piece of wreckage

79. **retention:** holding back

80. **All ... dedication:** i.e., dedicating all (my love) to him

81. **pure:** purely, simply

82. **adverse:** hostile

For shallow draught and bulk unprizable,
With which such scatheful grapple did he make
With the most noble bottom of our fleet
That very envy and the tongue of loss
Cried fame and honor on him.—What's the matter?

FIRST OFFICER
Orsino, this is that Antonio
That took the *Phoenix* and her fraught from Candy,
And this is he that did the *Tiger* board
When your young nephew Titus lost his leg.
Here in the streets, desperate of shame and state,
In private brabble did we apprehend him.

VIOLA
He did me kindness, sir, drew on my side,
But in conclusion put strange speech upon me.
I know not what 'twas but distraction.

ORSINO
Notable pirate, thou saltwater thief,
What foolish boldness brought thee to their mercies
Whom thou, in terms so bloody and so dear,
Hast made thine enemies?

ANTONIO   Orsino, noble sir,
Be pleased that I shake off these names you give me.
Antonio never yet was thief or pirate,
Though, I confess, on base and ground enough,
Orsino's enemy. A witchcraft drew me hither.
That most ingrateful boy there by your side
From the rude sea's enraged and foamy mouth
Did I redeem; a wrack past hope he was.
His life I gave him and did thereto add
My love, without retention or restraint,
All his in dedication. For his sake
Did I expose myself, pure for his love,
Into the danger of this adverse town;
Drew to defend him when he was beset;

85. **Not meaning to:** i.e., choosing not to
86. **face . . . out:** shamelessly exclude . . . from
88. **While . . . wink:** i.e., in the time it takes to blink one's eyes
89. **recommended:** consigned, given
94. **No int'rim:** without interruption
102. **What . . . that:** i.e., what does my lord wish, except for that
104. **keep promise with:** i.e., keep your promise to
110. **fat, fulsome:** disgusting

Woman with a distaff. (1.3.100)
From Johann Engel, *Astrolabium* (1488).

Where, being apprehended, his false cunning
(Not meaning to partake with me in danger)   85
Taught him to face me out of his acquaintance
And grew a twenty years' removèd thing
While one would wink; denied me mine own purse,
Which I had recommended to his use
Not half an hour before.   90
VIOLA How can this be?
ORSINO, ⌜*to Antonio*⌝ When came he to this town?
ANTONIO
Today, my lord; and for three months before,
No int'rim, not a minute's vacancy,
Both day and night did we keep company.   95

Enter Olivia and Attendants.

ORSINO
Here comes the Countess. Now heaven walks on
  earth!—
But for thee, fellow: fellow, thy words are madness.
Three months this youth hath tended upon me—
But more of that anon. ⌜*To an Officer.*⌝ Take him   100
  aside.
OLIVIA
What would my lord, but that he may not have,
Wherein Olivia may seem serviceable?—
Cesario, you do not keep promise with me.
VIOLA Madam?   105
ORSINO Gracious Olivia—
OLIVIA
What do you say, Cesario?—Good my lord—
VIOLA
My lord would speak; my duty hushes me.
OLIVIA
If it be aught to the old tune, my lord,
It is as fat and fulsome to mine ear   110
As howling after music.

113. **constant:** steadfast, immovable
114. **uncivil:** cruel
115. **ingrate:** ungrateful; **unauspicious:** inauspicious, unfavorable
117. **tendered:** offered
120. **th' Egyptian thief:** an allusion to a novel by Heliodorus, in which the robber chief, threatened with death, tries to kill the woman he loves to prevent her being taken by another
122. **savors nobly:** i.e., smacks of nobility
123. **to nonregardance cast:** i.e., fail to take notice of
124. **that:** i.e., since
125. **screws:** twists
126. **Live you:** i.e., continue to live as
127. **minion:** darling
128. **tender:** regard, esteem
135. **jocund, apt:** jocundly, aptly (i.e., happily, readily)
136. **do you rest:** i.e., give you peace
141. **you witnesses above:** i.e., you heavenly powers
142. **tainting:** corrupting, injuring

ORSINO
  Still so cruel?
OLIVIA   Still so constant, lord.
ORSINO
  What, to perverseness? You, uncivil lady,
  To whose ingrate and unauspicious altars   115
  My soul the faithful'st off'rings have breathed out
  That e'er devotion tendered—what shall I do?
OLIVIA
  Even what it please my lord that shall become him.
ORSINO
  Why should I not, had I the heart to do it,
  Like to th' Egyptian thief at point of death,   120
  Kill what I love?—a savage jealousy
  That sometimes savors nobly. But hear me this:
  Since you to nonregardance cast my faith,
  And that I partly know the instrument
  That screws me from my true place in your favor,   125
  Live you the marble-breasted tyrant still.
  But this your minion, whom I know you love,
  And whom, by heaven I swear, I tender dearly,
  Him will I tear out of that cruel eye
  Where he sits crownèd in his master's spite.—   130
  Come, boy, with me. My thoughts are ripe in mischief.
  I'll sacrifice the lamb that I do love
  To spite a raven's heart within a dove.
VIOLA
  And I, most jocund, apt, and willingly,   135
  To do you rest a thousand deaths would die.
OLIVIA
  Where goes Cesario?
VIOLA   After him I love
  More than I love these eyes, more than my life,
  More by all mores than e'er I shall love wife.   140
  If I do feign, you witnesses above,
  Punish my life for tainting of my love.

143. **beguiled:** cheated, deceived
151. **sirrah:** a term of address that, here, emphasizes the speaker's authority
153. **baseness:** contemptibleness, ignobleness
154. **strangle thy propriety:** i.e., conceal what you are; or, perhaps, hide the fact that I belong to you
156. **that:** that which (i.e., my husband)
157. **that thou fear'st:** i.e., Orsino **that:** that which
160. **unfold:** disclose
163. **newly:** recently
165. **joinder:** joining
166. **close:** union

Lucrece. (2.5.95)
From Silvestro Pietrasanta, *Symbola heroica* . . . (1682).

OLIVIA
Ay me, detested! How am I beguiled!
VIOLA
Who does beguile you? Who does do you wrong?
OLIVIA
Hast thou forgot thyself? Is it so long?— 145
Call forth the holy father. ⌜*An Attendant exits.*⌝
ORSINO, ⌜*to Viola*⌝ Come, away!
OLIVIA
Whither, my lord?—Cesario, husband, stay.
ORSINO
Husband?
OLIVIA   Ay, husband. Can he that deny? 150
ORSINO
Her husband, sirrah?
VIOLA   No, my lord, not I.
OLIVIA
Alas, it is the baseness of thy fear
That makes thee strangle thy propriety.
Fear not, Cesario. Take thy fortunes up. 155
Be that thou know'st thou art, and then thou art
As great as that thou fear'st.

Enter Priest.

O, welcome, father.
Father, I charge thee by thy reverence
Here to unfold (though lately we intended 160
To keep in darkness what occasion now
Reveals before 'tis ripe) what thou dost know
Hath newly passed between this youth and me.
PRIEST
A contract of eternal bond of love,
Confirmed by mutual joinder of your hands, 165
Attested by the holy close of lips,
Strengthened by interchangement of your rings,
And all the ceremony of this compact

169. **Sealed . . . function:** ratified by me in my role as priest

173. **dissembling:** hypocritical

174. **a grizzle:** gray hair; **case:** skin

175. **craft:** craftiness

176. **trip:** wrestling move in which one trips one's opponent

181. **Hold little:** i.e., keep a bit of

183. **presently:** immediately

185. **Has . . . across:** i.e., he has cut my head

186. **coxcomb:** i.e., head

191–92. **incardinate:** a mistake for "incarnate"

194. **'Od's lifelings:** by God's little lives

199. **bespake . . . fair:** addressed . . . courteously

The dormouse. (3.2.18)
From Edward Topsell, *The historie of foure-footed beastes . . .* (1607).

    Sealed in my function, by my testimony;
    Since when, my watch hath told me, toward my grave
    I have traveled but two hours.
ORSINO [*to Viola*]
    O thou dissembling cub! What wilt thou be
    When time hath sowed a grizzle on thy case?
    Or will not else thy craft so quickly grow
    That thine own trip shall be thine overthrow?
    Farewell, and take her, but direct thy feet
    Where thou and I henceforth may never meet.
VIOLA
    My lord, I do protest—
OLIVIA   O, do not swear.
    Hold little faith, though thou hast too much fear.

Enter Sir Andrew.

ANDREW   For the love of God, a surgeon! Send one presently to Sir Toby.
OLIVIA   What's the matter?
ANDREW   Has broke my head across, and has given Sir Toby a bloody coxcomb too. For the love of God, your help! I had rather than forty pound I were at home.
OLIVIA   Who has done this, Sir Andrew?
ANDREW   The Count's gentleman, one Cesario. We took him for a coward, but he's the very devil incardinate.
ORSINO   My gentleman Cesario?
ANDREW   'Od's lifelings, here he is!—You broke my head for nothing, and that that I did, I was set on to do 't by Sir Toby.
VIOLA
    Why do you speak to me? I never hurt you.
    You drew your sword upon me without cause,
    But I bespake you fair and hurt you not.

201. **set nothing by:** think nothing of
202. **halting:** limping
203. **in drink:** drunk
204. **othergates:** otherwise
206. **That's all one:** i.e., it doesn't matter
209. **set:** perhaps, closed; or, fixed; or, sunk out of sight
210. **passy-measures pavin:** perhaps a comment on the surgeon's slowness (**A pavin** is a stately dance, and the Italian word *passamezzo* means a slow tune.)
215. **dressed:** i.e., have our wounds dressed
216. **coxcomb:** fool; literally, the cap worn by a Fool (See page 176.)
220. **the ... blood:** i.e., my own brother
221. **with wit and safety:** i.e., with reasonable regard for my safety
222. **throw ... me:** look at me strangely (or, perhaps, coldly)
225. **so late ago:** so recently
226. **habit:** outfit
227. **A ... perspective:** i.e., an optical illusion created naturally, without mirrors or other optical devices (**perspectives**)

ANDREW If a bloody coxcomb be a hurt, you have hurt 200
me. I think you set nothing by a bloody coxcomb.

Enter Toby and ⌜Feste, the Fool.⌝

Here comes Sir Toby halting. You shall hear
more. But if he had not been in drink, he would
have tickled you othergates than he did.
ORSINO How now, gentleman? How is 't with you? 205
TOBY That's all one. Has hurt me, and there's th' end
on 't. ⌜*To Fool.*⌝ Sot, didst see Dick Surgeon, sot?
FOOL O, he's drunk, Sir Toby, an hour agone; his eyes
were set at eight i' th' morning.
TOBY Then he's a rogue and a passy-measures pavin. I 210
hate a drunken rogue.
OLIVIA Away with him! Who hath made this havoc
with them?
ANDREW I'll help you, Sir Toby, because we'll be
dressed together. 215
TOBY Will you help?—an ass-head, and a coxcomb,
and a knave, a thin-faced knave, a gull?
OLIVIA
Get him to bed, and let his hurt be looked to.
⌜*Toby, Andrew, Fool, and Fabian exit.*⌝

Enter Sebastian.

SEBASTIAN
I am sorry, madam, I have hurt your kinsman,
But, had it been the brother of my blood, 220
I must have done no less with wit and safety.
You throw a strange regard upon me, and by that
I do perceive it hath offended you.
Pardon me, sweet one, even for the vows
We made each other but so late ago. 225
ORSINO
One face, one voice, one habit, and two persons!
A natural perspective, that is and is not!

229. racked: The **rack** was an instrument of torture that tore the body apart. (See page 180.)

232. Fear'st thou: i.e., are you in doubt about

238–39. Nor . . . everywhere: i.e., nor do I have the power to be omnipresent, like a god

241. Of charity: i.e., out of kindness (i.e., please tell me)

245. suited: dressed

246. suit: clothing

249–50. am . . . participate: i.e., am the same flesh-and-blood creature that I've been from my birth **dimension:** bodily form **grossly:** materially **clad:** dressed **participate:** possess

251. as . . . even: i.e., since everything else fits together

A fool wearing a coxcomb. (5.1.216)
From George Wither, *A collection of emblemes . . .* (1635).

SEBASTIAN
Antonio, O, my dear Antonio!
How have the hours racked and tortured me
Since I have lost thee!   230
ANTONIO
Sebastian are you?
SEBASTIAN   Fear'st thou that, Antonio?
ANTONIO
How have you made division of yourself?
An apple cleft in two is not more twin
Than these two creatures. Which is Sebastian?   235
OLIVIA Most wonderful!
SEBASTIAN, ⌜*looking at Viola*⌝
Do I stand there? I never had a brother,
Nor can there be that deity in my nature
Of here and everywhere. I had a sister,
Whom the blind waves and surges have devoured.   240
Of charity, what kin are you to me?
What countryman? What name? What parentage?
VIOLA
Of Messaline. Sebastian was my father.
Such a Sebastian was my brother, too.
So went he suited to his watery tomb.   245
If spirits can assume both form and suit,
You come to fright us.
SEBASTIAN   A spirit I am indeed,
But am in that dimension grossly clad
Which from the womb I did participate.   250
Were you a woman, as the rest goes even,
I should my tears let fall upon your cheek
And say "Thrice welcome, drownèd Viola."
VIOLA
My father had a mole upon his brow.
SEBASTIAN And so had mine.   255
VIOLA
And died that day when Viola from her birth
Had numbered thirteen years.

258. **record:** memory (accent on second syllable)

261. **lets:** hinders

262. **But . . . attire:** except for the male clothing I have appropriated

264. **cohere, jump:** agree

267. **maiden weeds:** woman's clothing; **gentle:** kind, courteous

271. **mistook:** mistaken

272. **nature . . . that:** i.e., nature caused your desire, mistakenly directed to Viola, to swerve to me (The **bias** is the curve that brings the ball to the desired point in the game of bowls. See page 182.)

275. **maid and man:** i.e., a man who is a virgin

277. **the glass seems true:** i.e., the **perspective** glass seems to be representing the truth rather than a distortion

278. **wrack:** wreck, shipwreck; or, that which has washed up from the shipwreck

280. **like to me:** i.e., as much as you love me

281. **overswear:** i.e., swear over again

283. **that orbèd continent:** i.e., the sun (A **continent** is a container; the sun is pictured as containing fire.)

SEBASTIAN
  O, that record is lively in my soul!
  He finishèd indeed his mortal act
  That day that made my sister thirteen years.

VIOLA
  If nothing lets to make us happy both
  But this my masculine usurped attire,
  Do not embrace me till each circumstance
  Of place, time, fortune, do cohere and jump
  That I am Viola; which to confirm,
  I'll bring you to a captain in this town,
  Where lie my maiden weeds; by whose gentle help
  I was preserved to serve this noble count.
  All the occurrence of my fortune since
  Hath been between this lady and this lord.

SEBASTIAN, ⌜*to Olivia*⌝
  So comes it, lady, you have been mistook.
  But nature to her bias drew in that.
  You would have been contracted to a maid.
  Nor are you therein, by my life, deceived:
  You are betrothed both to a maid and man.

ORSINO, ⌜*to Olivia*⌝
  Be not amazed; right noble is his blood.
  If this be so, as yet the glass seems true,
  I shall have share in this most happy wrack.—
  Boy, thou hast said to me a thousand times
  Thou never shouldst love woman like to me.

VIOLA
  And all those sayings will I overswear,
  And all those swearings keep as true in soul
  As doth that orbèd continent the fire
  That severs day from night.

ORSINO   Give me thy hand,
  And let me see thee in thy woman's weeds.

VIOLA
  The Captain that did bring me first on shore

288. **upon some action:** as a result of legal action
289. **in durance:** imprisoned
291. **He ... him:** i.e., Malvolio shall free the captain
293. **remember me:** i.e., remember
294. **much distract:** quite mad
295. **extracting frenzy:** a temporary insanity that drew everything from my mind (except thoughts of Cesario)
296. **his:** i.e., Malvolio's "frenzy"
298-99. **he ... end:** i.e., he keeps the devil at a distance
300-1. **today morning:** i.e., this morning
302. **skills not much:** makes little difference
305. **delivers:** reads the words of
310. **allow vox:** permit me to use the appropriate "voice"
313. **thus:** i.e., like a madman; **perpend:** ponder, consider

Men being "racked." (5.1.229)
From Girolamo Maggi, *De tintinnabulis liber ... Accedit ... De equulet liber ...* (1689).

Hath my maid's garments. He, upon some action,
Is now in durance at Malvolio's suit,
A gentleman and follower of my lady's.
OLIVIA
He shall enlarge him.

Enter ⌜Feste, the Fool⌝ with a letter, and Fabian.

Fetch Malvolio hither.
And yet, alas, now I remember me,
They say, poor gentleman, he's much distract.
A most extracting frenzy of mine own
From my remembrance clearly banished his.
⌜*To the Fool.*⌝ How does he, sirrah?
FOOL Truly, madam, he holds Beelzebub at the stave's end as well as a man in his case may do. Has here writ a letter to you. I should have given 't you today morning. But as a madman's epistles are no gospels, so it skills not much when they are delivered.
OLIVIA Open 't and read it.
FOOL Look then to be well edified, when the Fool delivers the madman. ⌜*He reads.*⌝ *By the Lord, madam—*
OLIVIA How now, art thou mad?
FOOL No, madam, I do but read madness. An your Ladyship will have it as it ought to be, you must allow *vox.*
OLIVIA Prithee, read i' thy right wits.
FOOL So I do, madonna. But to read his right wits is to read thus. Therefore, perpend, my princess, and give ear.
OLIVIA, ⌜*giving letter to Fabian*⌝ Read it you, sirrah.
FABIAN (*reads*) *By the Lord, madam, you wrong me, and the world shall know it. Though you have put me into darkness and given your drunken cousin rule over me, yet have I the benefit of my senses as well as your Ladyship. I have your own letter that induced me to*

321. **the which:** i.e., **your own letter**
329. **delivered:** released
330–32. **so . . . wife:** i.e., if you are willing, once we've thought more about these things, to think as well of me as a sister-in-law as you were thinking of me as a wife
333. **crown . . . on 't:** i.e., celebrate the alliance that will make us kin (i.e., you can marry Viola at the same time I marry Sebastian)
335. **at my proper cost:** i.e., at my expense
336. **apt:** ready
337. **quits:** releases
339. **mettle:** nature
340. **breeding:** upbringing

The game of bowls. (5.1.272)
From *Le centre de l'amour* (1650).

182

> *the semblance I put on, with the which I doubt not but
> to do myself much right or you much shame. Think of
> me as you please. I leave my duty a little unthought of
> and speak out of my injury.*
>   *The madly used Malvolio.* 325

OLIVIA Did he write this?
FOOL Ay, madam.
ORSINO
This savors not much of distraction.
OLIVIA
See him delivered, Fabian. Bring him hither.
⌜*Fabian exits.*⌝
⌜*To Orsino.*⌝ My lord, so please you, these things 330
further thought on,
To think me as well a sister as a wife,
One day shall crown th' alliance on 't, so please
you,
Here at my house, and at my proper cost. 335
ORSINO
Madam, I am most apt t' embrace your offer.
⌜*To Viola.*⌝ Your master quits you; and for your
service done him,
So much against the mettle of your sex,
So far beneath your soft and tender breeding, 340
And since you called me "master" for so long,
Here is my hand. You shall from this time be
Your master's mistress.
OLIVIA, ⌜*to Viola*⌝   A sister! You are she.

Enter Malvolio ⌜*and Fabian.*⌝

ORSINO
Is this the madman? 345
OLIVIA   Ay, my lord, this same.—
How now, Malvolio?
MALVOLIO   Madam, you have done me
wrong,
Notorious wrong. 350

353. **hand:** handwriting
354. **from it:** differently (from the way you wrote in the letter)
355. **invention:** composition
357. **in . . . honor:** i.e., with the moderation that should go with honor
358. **lights:** perhaps, signs
361. **lighter:** lesser
362. **acting this:** i.e., doing what you said
363. **suffered:** allowed
365. **geck, gull:** dupe
366. **invention:** i.e., plotting, scheming; **played on:** victimized
368. **the character:** my handwriting
371. **cam'st:** i.e., you came
372–73. **forms . . . were presupposed / Upon:** i.e., style . . . was prescribed for
374. **This . . . thee:** i.e., this plot has maliciously tricked you
375. **authors:** inventors
381. **wondered at:** See note to 4.3.3.
384–85. **Upon . . . him:** i.e., because of some rude and ill-mannered characteristics of his that made us dislike him

OLIVIA Have I, Malvolio? No.
MALVOLIO, ⌜*handing her a paper*⌝
Lady, you have. Pray you peruse that letter.
You must not now deny it is your hand.
Write from it if you can, in hand or phrase,
Or say 'tis not your seal, not your invention. 355
You can say none of this. Well, grant it then,
And tell me, in the modesty of honor,
Why you have given me such clear lights of favor?
Bade me come smiling and cross-gartered to you,
To put on yellow stockings, and to frown 360
Upon Sir Toby and the lighter people?
And, acting this in an obedient hope,
Why have you suffered me to be imprisoned,
Kept in a dark house, visited by the priest,
And made the most notorious geck and gull 365
That e'er invention played on? Tell me why.
OLIVIA
Alas, Malvolio, this is not my writing,
Though I confess much like the character.
But out of question, 'tis Maria's hand.
And now I do bethink me, it was she 370
First told me thou wast mad; then cam'st in smiling,
And in such forms which here were presupposed
Upon thee in the letter. Prithee, be content.
This practice hath most shrewdly passed upon thee.
But when we know the grounds and authors of it, 375
Thou shalt be both the plaintiff and the judge
Of thine own cause.
FABIAN Good madam, hear me speak,
And let no quarrel nor no brawl to come
Taint the condition of this present hour, 380
Which I have wondered at. In hope it shall not,
Most freely I confess, myself and Toby
Set this device against Malvolio here,
Upon some stubborn and uncourteous parts
We had conceived against him. Maria writ 385

386. **importance:** importuning, urgent request
388. **it was followed:** i.e., the plot was carried out
389. **pluck on:** induce
392. **baffled thee:** put you to shame
395. **interlude:** comedy
399. **whirligig:** continual whirling
405. **convents:** perhaps, is convenient for all
409. **so you shall be:** i.e., that's what I'll call you
410. **habits:** clothes
411. **mistress:** (1) the woman he loves; (2) the person he obeys; **fancy's:** love's
414. **toy:** trifle

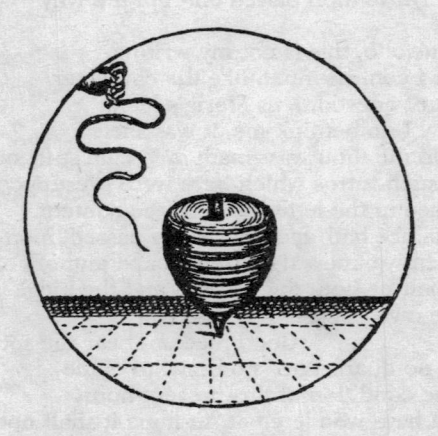

A top. (1.3.42)
From Giovanni Ferro, *Teatro imprese* . . . (1623).

> The letter at Sir Toby's great importance,
> In recompense whereof he hath married her.
> How with a sportful malice it was followed
> May rather pluck on laughter than revenge,
> If that the injuries be justly weighed   390
> That have on both sides passed.

OLIVIA, ⌜to Malvolio⌝
> Alas, poor fool, how have they baffled thee!

FOOL Why, "some are born great, some achieve greatness, and some have greatness thrown upon them."
I was one, sir, in this interlude, one Sir Topas, sir,   395
but that's all one. "By the Lord, Fool, I am not
mad"—but, do you remember "Madam, why laugh
you at such a barren rascal; an you smile not, he's
gagged"? And thus the whirligig of time brings in
his revenges.   400

MALVOLIO
> I'll be revenged on the whole pack of you! ⌜He exits.⌝

OLIVIA
> He hath been most notoriously abused.

ORSINO
> Pursue him and entreat him to a peace. ⌜Some exit.⌝
> He hath not told us of the Captain yet.
> When that is known, and golden time convents,   405
> A solemn combination shall be made
> Of our dear souls.—Meantime, sweet sister,
> We will not part from hence.—Cesario, come,
> For so you shall be while you are a man.
> But when in other habits you are seen,   410
> Orsino's mistress, and his fancy's queen.
>   ⌜All but the Fool⌝ exit.

FOOL sings
> *When that I was and a little tiny boy,*
>   *With hey, ho, the wind and the rain,*
> *A foolish thing was but a toy,*
>   *For the rain it raineth every day.*   415

416. **came . . . estate:** i.e., grew up to be a man
426. **tosspots:** drunkards (The meaning of this stanza continues to be debated.)
430. **that's all one:** i.e., none of that matters

"Arion on the dolphin's back." (1.2.16)
From Sigmund, freiherr von Herberstein, *Rerum Moscouiticarum commentarij . . . Russiae . . . descriptio . . .* (1556).

But when I came to man's estate,
　With hey, ho, the wind and the rain,
'Gainst knaves and thieves men shut their gate,
　For the rain it raineth every day.

But when I came, alas, to wive,
　With hey, ho, the wind and the rain,
By swaggering could I never thrive,
　For the rain it raineth every day.

But when I came unto my beds,
　With hey, ho, the wind and the rain,
With tosspots still had drunken heads,
　For the rain it raineth every day.

A great while ago the world begun,
　⌜*With*⌝ *hey, ho, the wind and the rain,*
But that's all one, our play is done,
　And we'll strive to please you every day.
　　　　　　　　　　　　　　⌜*He exits.*⌝

Textual Notes

The reading of the present text appears to the left of the square bracket. The earliest sources of readings not in **F,** the First Folio text (upon which this edition is based), are indicated as follows: **F2** is the Second Folio of 1632; **F3** is the Third Folio of 1663–64; **F4** is the Fourth Folio of 1685. **Ed.** is an earlier editor of Shakespeare, beginning with Rowe in 1709. No sources are given for emendations of punctuation or for corrections of obvious typographical errors, like turned letters that produce no known word. **SD** means stage direction; **SP** means speech prefix; **uncorr.** means the first or uncorrected state of the First Folio; **corr.** means the second or corrected state of the First Folio. ~ stands in place of a word already quoted before the square bracket; ∧ indicates the omission of a punctuation mark.

1.1	1. SP *and hereafter throughout* ORSINO] Ed.; *Duke* F (*"Duke."* or *"Du."* *throughout* F)
	10–11. capacity∧ ... sea, naught] ~, ... ~. ~ F
	24. SD *One-half line later in* F
	40. supplied, and] ~∧ ~ F
1.2	15. strong] sttong F
	16. Arion] Ed.; *Orion* F
1.3	1. SP TOBY] F (*Sir To.*)
	7 *and throughout.* SP TOBY] F (*To.*)
	36. moreover] moreour F
	51. SP ANDREW] F2; *Ma.* F
	54. Mary∧ Accost] Ed.; *Mary,* accost F
	97. will] willl F
	97. curl by] Ed.; coole my F
	99. me] F2; we F
	99. does 't] F (dost)

191

Twelfth Night

        105. Count] Connt F
        109. swear 't] swear˰t F
        113. kickshawses] F (kicke-chawses)
        132. dun-colored] Ed.; dam'd colour'd F
        132. set] Ed.; sit F
        136. That's] F3; That F

1.4   9. SD *one-half line earlier in* F; *Orsino*] Ed.; *Duke* F
        15. the] rhe F

1.5   0. SD *Feste, the Fool*] this ed.; *Clowne* F 5 *and throughout.* SP FOOL] this ed.; *Clo.* F
        86. gagged] F (gag'd)
    90–91. guiltless] guitlesse F
        113. for—here he comes—one] ~˰ ~~~. ~ F
        114. SD *1 line earlier in* F
        157. peascod] F (pescod)
        165. SD *Viola*] F2; *Violenta* F
        179. I] F *catch-word; omit* F *dialogue*
        182. swear ˰ I] ~) ~ F
  204, 205. SP OLIVIA, VIOLA] Ed.; *speech continues as Viola's in* F
        308. County's] F (Countes)
        318. SD *She exits.*] *Finis, Actus primus.* F

2.1   19. heavens] Heanens F
2.2   3. sir. On] ~, ~ F
        31. our] F2; O F
        32. made of,] Ed.; made, if F

2.3.   2. *diluculo*] Ed.; *Deliculo* F
        14. drink. Marian] ~˰ ~ F
        14. SD *Feste, the Fool*] this ed.; *Clowne* F
        24. Queubus] *Quenbus* F
        79. Tillyvally! "Lady"!] tilly vally. Ladie, F
        133. Malvolio] Malnolio F
        134. a nayword] Ed.; an ayword F
        175. SD *1 line earlier in* F

Textual Notes 193

2.4	0. SD *Orsino*] Ed.; *Duke* F
	17. boy. If] ~, ~ F
	25. masterly.] ~, F
	47. SD *Feste, the Fool*] this ed.; *Clowne* F
	60. *Fly . . . fly*] Ed.; *Fye . . . fie* F
	62. *yew*] F (*Ew*)
	97. I] Ed.; It F
2.5	59. my—some] ~ ˄ ~ F
	90. her great] het great F
	101. *Lips, do*] ~ ˄ ~ F
	104. altered] alter d F
	117. staniel] Ed.; stallion F
	123. portend? If] ~, ~ F
	149. *born*] Ed.; become F
	149. *achieve*] F2; atcheeues F
	158. *thee*] thce F
	161–62. *fingers. Farewell*] ~ ˄ ~ F
	163. *The*] tht F
	163–64. *Fortunate-Unhappy. Daylight*] ~ ˄ ~ ˄ ~ F
	165. politic] pollticke F
	181. *dear*] deero F
	190. SD *1 line earlier in* F
	200. vitae] vite F
	212. SD *They exit.*] *Exeunt. Finis Actus secnndus* [*sic*] F
3.1	0. SD *Feste, the Fool*] this ed.; *Clowne* F
	8. king] F2; Kings F
	9. church] Chureh F
	58. come.] ~, F
	69. wise men, folly-fall'n] Ed.; wisemens folly falne F
	72. *vous*] *vou* F
	93. all ready] F (already)
	152. beautiful ˄] ~? F
	153. lip!] ~, F
3.2	7. thee] F3; the F

194   Twelfth Night

	35. him.] ~ ˌ F
3.3	8. travel] rrauel F
	16. thanks, and ever thanks; and oft] Ed.; thankes; and euer oft F
	21. sir.] ~, F
	22. night.] ~ ˌ F
	32. Th' offense] Th ˌ offence F
3.4	16. merry] metry F
	16. SD *2 lines earlier in* F
	21. Sad, lady?] ~ ˌ ~, F
	26. SP OLIVIA] F2; *Mal.* F
	60. let] ler F
	66. looked] look d F
	76. tang] langer F
	179. If] *To.* If F
	181. You . . . fit . . . for 't] Yon . . . sit . . . fot't F
	229. thee] F (the)
	274. promise, to] ~ ˌ ~ F
	325. SD *1 line earlier in* F
	395. O, prove true] oh proue ttue F
4.1	0. SD *Feste, the Fool*] this ed.; *Clowne* F
4.2	0. SD *Feste, the Fool*] this ed.; *Clowne* F
	6. in] in in F
12, 16, 29, 89.	Master] M. F
	15. Gorboduc] F (*Gorbodacke*)
	39. clerestories] Ed.; cleere stores F
	54. haply] F (happily)
	125. begone] be goue F
4.3	1. SP *omit* F
	37. SD *They exit.*] *Exeunt. Finis Actus Quartus.* F
5.1	0. SD *Feste, the Fool*] this ed.; *Clowne* F
	2. Master] M. F
	6. SD *Orsino*] Ed.; *Duke* F
	35. Saint] F (S.)

Textual Notes

188. home] homc F
191–92. incardinate] incardinatc F
201. SD *Feste, the Fool*] this ed.; *Clowne* F, where SD is 2 lines earlier
210. pavin] F (panyn)
216. help?—] ~ ͵ F
284. from] ftom F
291. SD *Feste, the Fool*] this ed.; *Clowne* F, where SD is 2 1/2 lines later
396. Lord] Lotd F
412. *tiny*] F (*tine*)
417, 421, 425. *With hey, ho, the wind and the rain*] Ed.; *with hey ho, &c.* F
419, 423, 427. *For the rain it raineth every day*] Ed.; *for the raine, &c.* F
428. begun] Ed.; *begon* F
429. *With hey, ho, the wind and the rain*] F2 (*which adds "With"*); *hey ho, &c.* F
431. SD *He exits.*] FINIS. F

Twelfth Night:
A Modern Perspective

Catherine Belsey

Who is it that Olivia falls in love with?[1]

In Act 1, scene 5 of *Twelfth Night*, the self-imposed seclusion of the Lady Olivia, in mourning for her brother, whose death has left her in control of an aristocratic household, is disrupted by the latest in a succession of messengers pressing the suit of Duke Orsino. This messenger, more insistent than all the others, brooks no denial and demands access to her. Olivia, curious, is equally insistent that Malvolio should describe the messenger: "What kind o' man is he? . . . What manner of man? . . . Of what personage and years is he?" (1.5.149–54). Malvolio's reply points to a certain elusiveness in the messenger's identity, defining Cesario primarily in terms of what he is not:

> Not yet old enough for a man, nor young enough for a boy—as a squash is before 'tis a peascod, or a codling when 'tis almost an apple. 'Tis with him in standing water, between boy and man. He is very well-favored, and he speaks very shrewishly. One would think his mother's milk were scarce out of him.   (1.5.155–61)

Orsino's messenger is identifiable by the traces he bears of other identities that are not his own: not quite a man, not exactly a boy; at the same time he evokes something of the feminine by his high-pitched voice, and perhaps a vestige of his mother's milk. There is a certain indeterminacy here. The veiled Olivia, traditional Petrarchan lady, aloof and mysterious, herself until now the object of Orsino's and the audience's curiosity, is caught and held by another mystery, the undecidable identity of her suitor's representative.

It is important, of course, for the audience to be reminded that Cesario is a woman in disguise, especially in an all-male theater, where the part was played by a male actor. And it is important too that we should know the disguise is effective. But this is not the first time that the play has dwelt on the elusiveness of Cesario's sexual identity. Orsino tells him:

> . . . they shall yet belie thy happy years
> That say thou art a man. Diana's lip
> Is not more smooth and rubious, thy small pipe
> Is as the maiden's organ, shrill and sound,
> And all is semblative a woman's part.
> (1.4.33–37)

Ironically, Orsino too, though he does not yet know it, is in the process of falling in love. Here again Cesario is not, we are to understand, a man. He resembles a woman, but he is not quite that either. His voice is *as* a maiden's. He is *like* Diana, goddess of chastity, perpetual virgin, who passed her time hunting in the forest and was the least stereotypically feminine of the female immortals.

Each time, some quality evades the speakers in these definitions, and the romantic comedy depends on the elusiveness of Viola-Cesario's sexual identity. Olivia falls in love with Cesario, but Viola cannot love Olivia. Orsino apparently fails to fall in love with Cesario, and Viola loves Orsino. From the point of view of the audience, this double dramatic irony, and the uncertainty about how the play will untangle the love knots it has tied, constitutes much of the pleasure of the romantic story.

A Modern Perspective   199

The shipwrecked Viola, frustrated in her initial desire to seek employment with Olivia, resolves to present herself to Orsino as a eunuch, since she is skilled in music. (Ladies could properly become companions to other ladies, but the household of an unmarried man offered no scope for ladies-in-waiting.) In Terence's Roman comedy, *The Eunuch* (almost certainly familiar to Shakespeare from the grammar-school curriculum[2]), Chaerea, defined in the English translation of 1598 as a "stripling," disguises himself in the clothes of a eunuch in order to gain entry to a household which includes the woman he loves. His value to the lady of the house is his skill in literature, athletics, and music. Once alone with the object of his desire, however, Chaerea promptly rapes her, and his cover is blown.

Terence's play thus gives very little idea of what eunuchs might usefully do once they took up residence as members of a household. Cesario's role as a eunuch is not referred to again. In practice he is treated as a page, and it is the Fool who does the singing. But something of the indeterminacy of the eunuch invests Viola to the end of the play, where Orsino continues to call her Cesario, and defers beyond the edges of the fiction the moment when she will change back into a woman's dress and become "Orsino's mistress, and his fancy's queen" (5.1.411).

While the male-female body of Cesario-Viola is repeatedly set before us by the words of the text, its undecidability would have been materially underlined for Shakespeare's audience by the body of the male actor. It is very difficult to reconstruct the experience of an audience accustomed to an all-male theater, where women's parts were always played by men or boys. Probably for much of the time the sex of the actor was irrelevant. No doubt in general the audience simply entered into the illusion created by the fiction, without forgetting, any more than we do, that it *was* an illusion. The body of Olivia, for instance, is not in question (though that role, too, was played by a boy), and her body is described as perfectly feminine in the most conventional sense: " . . . beauty truly blent, whose red and white / Nature's own sweet and cunning hand laid on" (1.5.238–39).

Orsino, meanwhile, is equally conventionally handsome. Even Olivia concedes that he is "in dimension and the shape of nature / A gracious person" (1.5.263–64). These ideal romance protagonists are in direct contrast to the grotesque bodies that surround them: Sir Toby Belch, whose name and perpetual revelry probably indicate a resemblance to the gross allegorical figure of Gluttony; Sir Andrew Aguecheek, Toby's antithesis, a puny "manikin" (3.2.52) whose thin, stringy hair "hangs like flax on a distaff" (1.3.100); and above all, of course, Malvolio, dressed up for Olivia's benefit, absurd in outmoded yellow stockings, cross-gartered, and smiling relentlessly.

Each of these bodies proclaims an identity. Only Viola-Cesario's physical form specifies an enigma. Is it this which constitutes her/him as an object of desire for Olivia? Certainly Cesario's body is not a matter of indifference to Olivia:

> "I am a gentleman." I'll be sworn thou art.
> Thy tongue, thy face, thy limbs, actions, and spirit
> Do give thee fivefold blazon . . .
> . . . How now? . . .
> Methinks I feel this youth's perfections
> With an invisible and subtle stealth
> To creep in at mine eyes.   (1.5.296–304)

In the event, since marriage is the issue, Viola's body will not do. Sebastian's apparently identical but this time unequivocally masculine body will prove more adequate, and equally desirable.

And yet Cesario's body is not, for Olivia, the whole story. "Thy tongue, thy face, thy limbs, actions, and spirit . . .": these are the features that both show Cesario to be a gentleman and constitute his seductive perfections. They include his behavior, his "spirit" (something much less material: a disposition, a temperament, an animating principle), and perhaps above all his "tongue," his way of speaking, probably, rather than the organ itself, Cesario's eloquence and his wit. And here too Olivia repeatedly identifies a certain elusiveness, an enigma which she tries—and fails—to resolve. Cesario begins his address to her in the grand style: "Most radiant, exquisite, and unmatchable beauty. . . ." But no sooner has he begun than he draws attention to the absurdity of such rhetoric aimed anonymously:

> I pray you, tell me if this be the lady of the house, for I never saw her. I would be loath to cast away my speech, for, besides that it is excellently well penned, I have taken great pains to con it.
>
> (1.5.169–72)

Cesario here speaks initially as if from the place of Orsino, whose representative he is, and then shifts, within the sentence, to the position of the messenger, comically going on to betray that the "message" is of his own making. Who, then, is the "author" of Cesario's words?

Olivia's response can be seen as an indirect attempt to elicit an answer to that question, to locate the *origin* of what Cesario says: "Whence came you, sir?"; and then, since the answer is an evasion, she asks, "Are you a comedian [an actor]?" (175, 180). Cesario denies it, naturally, but then goes on, "And yet . . . I swear I am not that

I play" (181–82). Who is speaking now? Not Cesario, but Viola, of course. But is this simply the Viola who is a woman pretending to be a man? Or is it more specifically the Viola who is a substitute for Orsino, pretending on his behalf to represent him, *re-presenting* his love for Olivia, when she is herself in love with Orsino?

Cesario presses Olivia to declare herself the lady of the house, and Olivia is able to reply with a quibble that only establishes more firmly her identity in the fiction: "If I do not usurp myself, I am" (184). She speaks from a single place. But Viola occupies a whole range of subject positions in rapid succession, and perhaps it is this above all that constitutes her as an enigma, and correspondingly as an object of desire, not only for the characters in the play but also, in a sense, for the audience.

"If I did love you in my master's flame," Viola-Cesario tells Olivia, I would not acknowledge or accept your rejection. "Why," Olivia asks, "what would you?" (1.5.266–70). What does Olivia want to hear? Not about Orsino, of course, but what Cesario would do if *he* loved her. And what does the audience hear as Viola replies non-ironically, lyrically, but conditionally, about love's insistent, repetitive *naming* of the beloved?

> Make me a willow cabin at your gate
> And call upon my soul within the house,
> Write loyal cantons of contemnèd love
> And sing them loud even in the dead of night,
> Hallow your name to the reverberate hills
> And make the babbling gossip of the air
> Cry out "Olivia!"   (1.5.271–77)

Who is speaking here? Cesario, loyally affirming Orsino's love? Yes, in a sense. Or Viola declaring her own love for Orsino? Yes and no: the name that Echo repeats is "Olivia," but then Echo can only repeat the speech of another; its origin is a matter of indifference to her. Or is it a voice beyond either, which is the condition of the possibility of Orsino's love and Viola's, and of our uncertainty about which is in question here, the strangely impersonal, shared because culturally specified, and thus always in one sense *echoed* voice of love "itself"?

A similar indeterminacy informs Viola-Cesario's history of her-his father's daughter, who pined for love like Patience on a monument (2.4.122–30). It is too easy to ascribe this account to Viola herself. As a story of any unrequited love, recounted by a woman who is shown within the fiction to be exceptionally active, busy, and witty, this both is and is not Viola's own story: "I am all the daughters of my father's house, / And all the brothers, too—and yet I know not" (2.4.132–33).

Viola, who is named only once, very late in the text (5.1.253), has no fixed location in the play. Even when she speaks "in her own person"—and it is not easy to be sure when that is—the play does not always make clear where we are to find "her" identity. In this sense she acts as a figure for the desire that circulates in the play. Though Viola's own desire is constant, the desire of the others keeps moving: from Olivia to Cesario, and on to Sebastian; from Orsino to Olivia, and then on to Viola. If it finds a fixed place in Act 5, perhaps arbitrarily, that may be simply because the play must end, and romantic comedies traditionally end in marriage. The objects of desire, the play implies, are in some senses interchangeable, so that Sebastian can easily take the place of Cesario, Viola of Olivia. Love itself invests the object with value. As a love story *Twelfth Night* is remarkably unsentimental about the romances it depicts with such sympathy.

Viola's counterpart outside the love story is the Fool, who is named Feste only once (2.4.12), and who equally has no fixed place to be. He was Olivia's father's jester, but he is also to be found at Orsino's court, moving easily between the two, just as Viola does. And he too is emblematic, a figure for the folly that also circulates in the play, since "Foolery . . . does walk about the orb like the sun; it shines everywhere" (3.1.40–41). Folly motivates the world of the comic subplot. It is to be found in the late-night carousing of Sir Toby Belch and his cronies. It is especially evident in the deportment of Sir Andrew Aguecheek, the "foolish knight" who solemnly declares, "Methinks sometimes I have no more wit than a Christian or an ordinary man has. But I am a great eater of beef, and I believe that does harm to my wit" (1.3.83–86). (It would be worth counting the number of absurdities in that utterance alone.) And folly is displayed supremely in the narcissistic posturings of Malvolio, who loves for advancement, and who knows how to do so only according to the letter.

But folly also inhabits the world of romance, or so the Fool assures us. Olivia, he argues, "will keep no Fool, sir, till she be married, and Fools are as like husbands as pilchers are to herrings: the husband's the bigger (3.1.35–37). And yet, he slyly indicates to Cesario, the foolery of love already inhabits Olivia's house as commonly as it accompanies Orsino—and it is Cesario (ironically addressed as "your Wisdom") who provokes it: "I would be sorry, sir, but the Fool should be as oft with your master as with my mistress. I think I saw your Wisdom there" (3.1.41–43).

The Fool works with words. They are his living. He invests their carnivalesque duplicity with materiality and makes money out of them. Folly throws into relief the ways in which language is opaque rather than transparent, an end and not a means. The Fool exploits the anarchic instability of meaning, introducing by a pun, a double entendre, or an equivocation an unexpected sense which obscures what is predictable and produces unforeseen significances. To Olivia's "Take the Fool away," he replies, "Take away the Lady," and justifies his case (1.5.36–70). Words, his foolery demonstrates, live a life of their own, independent of the intentions of his interlocutors.

But in this respect, too, folly is only the degree zero of courtship, where Malvolio, at the mercy of the letter, closely resembles Sir Andrew, who actively scoops up Cesario's fine phrases in order to put them to work on his own behalf. Love's script is always already written in advance, and the lover can do no more than put together a text and a mode of behavior from the existing repertoire. Both Malvolio and Sir Andrew may be seen as parodies of Orsino in love, aimlessly punning and poeticizing in the absence of the object of his desire. "Love," Julia Kristeva proposes, "is something spoken, and it is only that: poets have always known it."[3] The play does not go quite that far, but it points to the way the world of love inhabits the world of words—and shares in the process their anarchic, unstable, arbitrary nature.

Paradoxically, it follows that the work of the Fool (like the work of the dramatist?) is highly skilled, since it takes advantage of this anarchic character without submitting to it. Moreover, foolery (like drama?) is a discipline involving a strong awareness of what is appropriate. Folly (like the stage?) is licensed to say what might not be acceptable in another mode (1.5.92–93), but it also confronts quite stringent constraints:

> This fellow is wise enough to play the Fool,
> And to do that well craves a kind of wit.
> He must observe their mood on whom he jests,
> The quality of persons, and the time,
> And, like the haggard, check at every feather
> That comes before his eye. This is a practice
> As full of labor as a wise man's art. . . .
>
> (3.1.61–67)

The Fool, who is independent of the love story, draws the attention of the audience to the absurdity of love, even while the romantic narrative enlists our sympathy. By turns lyrical, sad, and ridiculous, love in *Twelfth Night* shares something of the elusiveness which characterizes the play's cross-dressed protagonist. It never settles in a single place long enough for us to feel that we have resolved its enigmas or eliminated its indeterminacies. And this is perhaps one of the effects of romantic comedy, which constantly shifts the perspective it offers its audience. The spectators of *Twelfth Night* are at one moment detached observers of love's extravagance and its self-indulgence, while at another they are invited to participate in its pains and pleasures, sharing the point of view of the fictional lovers themselves.

The truth about love, beyond its enigmas and its uncertainties, perhaps ultimately constitutes an unattainable object of desire for the audience of *Twelfth Night*. But so too, possibly, does the world of the fiction itself, a world of romance and foolery, of lyric and comedy. And here it is, of course, the Fool who has the last word. As *Twelfth Night*, the culminating party of the festive Christmas season, comes to an end, as the illusory realm of Illyria, constructed primarily out of language's imaginary transparency, recedes, the Fool, alone on the stage, sings a sad song about time and winter. Here in the margins of the fiction, a figure from the world made of words that is already lost to the audience defines an alternative world of wind and rain.

But that world is also made of words. Is it, we might wonder, more, or less, substantial than the realm of desire identified as Illyria?

---

1. This essay took shape in the course of conversations with Kent Cartwright, Barbara Mowat, Lena

Orlin, and Elihu Pearlman. It owes much to their insights.

2. "I believe we can say that Shakespere knew *Eunuchus*, and that of Terence's plays it was his favorite," writes T. W. Baldwin, who cites a number of allusions to *The Eunuch* in Shakespeare's work, but does not mention *Twelfth Night*. See *Shakespere's Five-Act Structure* (Urbana, Ill.: University of Illinois Press, 1947), pp. 544–78, esp. p. 576.

3. Julia Kristeva, *Tales of Love*, trans. Leon S. Roudiez (New York: Columbia University Press, 1987), p. 277.

Further Reading

Twelfth Night

Barber, C. L. "Testing Courtesy and Humanity in *Twelfth Night*." In *Shakespeare's Festive Comedy*, pp. 240–61. Princeton: Princeton University Press, 1959.

Barber's well-known essay treats the festive spirit implied in the play's title. Malvolio's presence is appropriate in this sense, for he acts as a foreign body that must be expelled by laughter. By moving the audience through release to clarification, the play explores the powers in human nature that make good the risks of social courtesy and liberty displayed in Viola's character.

Belsey, Catherine. "Disrupting Sexual Difference: Meaning and Gender in the Comedies." In *Alternative Shakespeares*, edited by John Drakakis, pp. 166–90. London: Methuen, 1985.

By disrupting the difference between masculine and feminine, Shakespeare's comedies radically challenge patriarchal values. As one instance, Belsey pursues the way *Twelfth Night* unfixes gender distinctions toward comic, romantic ends. *Twelfth Night*'s ending depends on the closing off of "glimpsed transgression" and the reinstatement of a clearly defined sexual distinction. But, as Belsey reminds us, "plays are more than their endings."

Brown, John Russell. "Directions for *Twelfth Night, or What You Will*." In *Shakespeare's Plays in Performance*, pp. 207–19. New York: St. Martin's, 1967.

For Brown, *Twelfth Night* poses a greater challenge to the theatrical practitioner than most plays. Exploring possible solutions that will answer the demands of both the text *and* the modern stage, Brown imagines a production that would bring together the varied elements of the Illyrian world, a world alternately—and often simultaneously—"gay, quiet, strained, solemn, dignified, elegant, easy, complicated, precarious, hearty, [and] homely. . . ."

Everett, Barbara. "Or What You Will." *Essays in Criticism* 35 (1985): 294–314.

Everett explores musicality, characterization, verbal style, the significance of the play's subtitle, and the role of Feste in response to what, for Everett, is the primary question posed by *Twelfth Night* and Shakespeare's earlier comedies: "Why do we take them seriously? Or how, rather, best to explore the ways in which it is hard *not* to take them seriously—the sense that at their best they achieve a lightness as far as possible from triviality."

Greenblatt, Stephen. "Fiction and Friction." In *Shakespearean Negotiations*, pp. 66–93. Berkeley: University of California Press, 1988.

Exploring his sense that *Twelfth Night* forever skirts illicit, homosexual desire, Greenblatt traces the course of the "swerving" necessary to avert social, theological, and legal disaster. By historicizing the sexual nature of Shakespeare's work within other social discourses of the body, Greenblatt establishes that, since women were understood to be inverted mirror images of men, there would be an inherent homoeroticism in all sexuality, although consummation of desire could be licitly figured only in the love of a man and a woman. It is this "mobility of desire" upon which the "delicious confusions of *Twelfth Night* depend. . . ."

Hartman, Geoffrey H. "Shakespeare's Poetical Character in *Twelfth Night*." In *Shakespeare and the Question of Theory*, edited by Geoffrey Hartman and Patricia Parker, pp. 37–53. London: Methuen, 1985.

Analyzing the ways Shakespeare's language, especially punning and wordplay, relates to character, Hartman examines the flux of language between real consequence—as in Malvolio's desperate pleas for release—and mere quibbling. *Twelfth Night* hints at moments of clarification ("Good madam, let me see your face") but defers pure revelation because the text, sustained by wit, keeps turning. According to Hartman, "There is always more to say."

Howard, Jean E. "Crossdressing, the Theatre, and Gender Struggle in Early Modern England." *Shakespeare Quarterly* 39 (1988): 418–40.

Howard uses preachers' and polemicists' attacks on cross dressing during the 1580–1620 period as signals of a sex-gender system under pressure to argue that cross dressing threatened the normative social order of hierarchy. But Howard argues that, in *Twelfth Night*, the cross-dressed Viola fails to challenge this social order, while Olivia powerfully challenges it.

Kermode, Frank. "The Mature Comedies." In *Early Shakespeare*, edited by John Russell Brown and Bernard Harris, pp. 211–27. Stratford-upon-Avon Studies 3. London: Edward Arnold, 1961.

Shakespeare's preoccupation with the comedy of mistaken identity takes subtlest form, for Kermode, in *Twelfth Night*, where the inability certainly to distinguish between what is meant and what is said, between things as they are and things as they appear to be, develops "a peculiar relevance to life itself." Kermode terms the play a "comedy of identity, set on the borders of wonder and madness."

Novy, Marianne. "'An You Smile Not, He's Gagged': Mutuality in Shakespeare's Comedy." In *Love's Argument: Gender Relations in Shakespeare*, pp. 21–44. Chapel Hill: University of North Carolina Press, 1984.

Novy follows the linguistic implications of "mutuality": the mutual dependence of romantic couples in Shakespeare's comic world. Marking the similarities of the suppliant lover and court jester—both depend for success upon a response of acceptance—Novy reads both wooing speeches and jokes as attempts to establish relationships. Shakespeare's most interesting comic lovers depend upon these verbal modes of interplay to develop their relationships. In this way, Shakespeare departs from both classical Roman comedy and the Petrarchan tradition in which "the focus is on the man, the initiator."

Rackin, Phyllis. "Androgyny, Mimesis, and the Marriage of the Boy Heroine on the English Renaissance Stages." *PMLA* 102 (1987): 29–47.

Rackin explores the changing conceptions of gender and theatrical mimesis through transvestite heroines in five English Renaissance plays, including *Twelfth Night*. Topics include the sexual ambiguity of the boy heroine in association with the problematic relationship between the male actor and the female character he plays, the dramatic action and the reality it imitates, and the play and the audience that watches it. The increasingly rigid gender distinctions and the devaluation of the feminine are associated with a rejection of fantasy and a deepening anxiety about theatrical representation.

Summers, Joseph. "The Masks of *Twelfth Night*." In *Shakespeare: Modern Essays in Criticism*, edited by Leonard F. Dean, pp. 134–43. Rev. ed. New York: Oxford: University Press, 1967.

Noting that in *Twelfth Night* the usual Shakespearean barrier to romantic fulfillment—a "responsible" older generation—has been abolished, Summers examines why the inhabitants of Illyria discover that they are anything but free. Summers removes the mask of each character, determining that most of them know "neither themselves, nor others, nor their social worlds." Within comedy, "we laugh with the characters who know the role they are playing and we laugh at those who do not." Summers divides the cast into those two broad categories but points out that the professional fool, Feste, "never makes the amateur's mistake of confusing his personality with his mask. . . ."

Shakespeare's Language

Abbott, E. A. *A Shakespearian Grammar.* New York: Haskell House, 1972.

This compact reference book, first published in 1870, helps with many difficulties in Shakespeare's language. It systematically accounts for a host of differences between Shakespeare's usage and sentence structure and our own.

Blake, Norman. *Shakespeare's Language: An Introduction.* New York: St. Martin's Press, 1983.

This general introduction to Elizabethan English discusses various aspects of the language of Shakespeare and his contemporaries, offering possible meanings for hundreds of ambiguous constructions.

Dobson, E. J. *English Pronunciation, 1500–1700.* 2 vols. Oxford: Clarendon Press, 1968.

This long and technical work includes chapters on

spelling (and its reformation), phonetics, stressed vowels, and consonants in early modern English.

Houston, John. *Shakespearean Sentences: A Study in Style and Syntax.* Baton Rouge: Louisiana State University Press, 1988.

Houston studies Shakespeare's stylistic choices, considering matters such as sentence length and the relative positions of subject, verb, and direct object. Examining plays throughout the canon in a roughly chronological, developmental order, he analyzes how sentence structure is used in setting tone, in characterization, and for other dramatic purposes.

Onions, C. T. *A Shakespeare Glossary.* Oxford: Clarendon Press, 1986.

This revised edition updates Onions's standard, selective glossary of words and phrases in Shakespeare's plays that are now obsolete, archaic, or obscure.

Partridge, Eric. *Shakespeare's Bawdy.* London: Routledge & Kegan Paul, 1955.

After an introductory essay, "The Sexual, the Homosexual, and Non-Sexual Bawdy in Shakespeare," Partridge provides a comprehensive glossary of "bawdy" phrases and words from the plays.

Robinson, Randal. *Unlocking Shakespeare's Language: Help for the Teacher and Student.* Urbana, Ill.: National Council of Teachers of English and the ERIC Clearinghouse on Reading and Communication Skills, 1989.

Specifically designed for the high-school and undergraduate college teacher and student, Robinson's book addresses the problems that most often hinder present-day readers of Shakespeare. Through work with his own students, Robinson found that many readers today are particularly puzzled by such stylistic characteristics as subject-verb inversion, interrupted structures, and compression. He shows how our own colloquial language contains comparable structures, and thus helps students recognize such structures when they find them in Shakespeare's plays. This book supplies worksheets—with examples from major plays—to illuminate and remedy such problems as unusual sequences of words and the separation of related parts of sentences.

Shakespeare's Life

Baldwin, T. W. *William Shakspere's Petty School.* Urbana: University of Illinois Press, 1943.

Baldwin here investigates the theory and practice of the petty school, the first level of education in Elizabethan England. He focuses on that educational system primarily as it is reflected in Shakespeare's art.

Baldwin, T. W. *William Shakspere's Small Latine and Lesse Greeke.* 2 vols. Urbana: University of Illinois Press, 1944.

Baldwin attacks the view that Shakespeare was an uneducated genius—a view that had been dominant among Shakespeareans since the eighteenth century. Instead, Baldwin shows, the educational system of Shakespeare's time would have given the playwright a strong background in the classics, and there is much in the plays that shows how Shakespeare benefited from such an education.

Beier, A. L., and Roger Finlay, eds. *London 1500–1700: The Making of the Metropolis.* New York: Longman, 1986.

Focusing on the economic and social history of early modern London, these collected essays probe aspects of metropolitan life, including "Population and Disease," "Commerce and Manufacture," and "Society and Change."

Bentley, G. E. *Shakespeare's Life: A Biographical Handbook.* New Haven: Yale University Press, 1961.

This "just-the-facts" account presents the surviving documents of Shakespeare's life against an Elizabethan background.

Chambers, E. K. *William Shakespeare: A Study of Facts and Problems.* 2 vols. Oxford: Clarendon Press, 1930.

Analyzing in great detail the scant historical data, Chambers's complex, scholarly study considers the nature of the texts in which Shakespeare's work is preserved.

Cressy, David. *Education in Tudor and Stuart England.* London: Edward Arnold, 1975.

This volume collects sixteenth-, seventeenth-, and early-eighteenth-century documents detailing aspects of formal education in England, such as the curriculum, the control and organization of education, and the education of women.

Dutton, Richard. *William Shakespeare: A Literary Life.* New York: St. Martin's Press, 1989.

Not a biography in the traditional sense, Dutton's very readable work nevertheless "follows the contours of Shakespeare's life" as he examines Shakespeare's career as playwright and poet, with consideration of his patrons, theatrical associations, and audience.

Fraser, Russell. *Young Shakespeare.* New York: Columbia University Press, 1988.

Fraser focuses on Shakespeare's first thirty years, paying attention simultaneously to his life and art.

De Grazia, Margreta. *Shakespeare Verbatim: The Reproduction of Authenticity and the Apparatus of 1790*. Oxford: Clarendon Press, 1991.

De Grazia traces and discusses the development of such editorial criteria as authenticity, historical periodization, factual biography, chronological developments, and close reading, locating as the point of origin Edmond Malone's 1790 edition of Shakespeare's works. There are interesting chapters on the First Folio and on the "legendary" versus the "documented" Shakespeare.

Schoenbaum, S. *William Shakespeare: A Compact Documentary Life*. New York: Oxford University Press, 1977.

This standard biography economically presents the essential documents from Shakespeare's time in an accessible narrative account of the playwright's life.

Shakespeare's Theater

Bentley, G. E. *The Profession of Player in Shakespeare's Time, 1590–1642*. Princeton: Princeton University Press, 1984.

Bentley readably sets forth a wealth of evidence about performance in Shakespeare's time, with special attention to the relations between player and company, and the business of casting, managing, and touring.

Berry, Herbert. *Shakespeare's Playhouses*. New York: AMS Press, 1987.

Berry's six essays collected here discuss (with illustrations) varying aspects of the four playhouses in which Shakespeare had a financial stake: the Theatre in Shoreditch, the Blackfriars, and the first and second Globe.

Cook, Ann Jennalie. *The Privileged Playgoers of Shakespeare's London*. Princeton: Princeton University Press, 1981.

Cook's work argues, on the basis of sociological, economic, and documentary evidence, that Shakespeare's audience—and the audience for English Renaissance drama generally—consisted mainly of the "privileged."

Greg, W. W. *Dramatic Documents from the Elizabethan Playhouses*. 2 vols. Oxford: Clarendon Press, 1931.

Greg itemizes and briefly describes almost all the play manuscripts that survive from the period 1590 to around 1660, including, among other things, players' parts. His second volume offers facsimiles of selected manuscripts.

Gurr, Andrew. *Playgoing in Shakespeare's London*. Cambridge: Cambridge University Press, 1987.

Gurr charts how the theatrical enterprise developed from its modest beginnings in the late 1560s to become a thriving institution in the 1600s. He argues that there were important changes over the period 1567–1644 in the playhouses, the audience, and the plays.

Harbage, Alfred. *Shakespeare's Audience*. New York: Columbia University Press, 1941.

Harbage investigates the fragmentary surviving evidence to interpret the size, composition, and behavior of Shakespeare's audience.

Hattaway, Michael. *Elizabethan Popular Theatre: Plays in Performance*. London: Routledge & Kegan Paul, 1982.

Beginning with a study of the popular drama of the late Elizabethan age—a description of the stages, performance conditions, and acting of the period—this volume concludes with an analysis of five well-known plays of the 1590s, one of them (*Titus Andronicus*) by Shakespeare.

Shapiro, Michael. *Children of the Revels: The Boy Companies of Shakespeare's Time and Their Plays*. New York: Columbia University Press, 1977.

Shapiro chronicles the history of the amateur and quasi-professional child companies that flourished in London at the end of Elizabeth's reign and the beginning of James's.

The Publication of Shakespeare's Plays

Blayney, Peter. *The First Folio of Shakespeare*. Hanover, Md.: Folger, 1991.

Blayney's accessible account of the printing and later life of the First Folio—an amply illustrated catalogue to a 1991 Folger Shakespeare Library exhibition—analyzes the mechanical production of the First Folio, describing how the Folio was made, by whom and for whom, how much it cost, and its ups and downs (or, rather, downs and ups) since its printing in 1623.

Hinman, Charlton. *The Printing and Proof-Reading of the First Folio of Shakespeare*. 2 vols. Oxford: Clarendon Press, 1963.

In the most arduous study of a single book ever undertaken, Hinman attempts to reconstruct how the Shakespeare First Folio of 1623 was set into type and run off the press, sheet by sheet. He also provides almost all the known variations in readings from copy to copy.

Hinman, Charlton. *The Norton Facsimile: The First Folio of Shakespeare.* New York: W. W. Norton, 1968.

This facsimile presents a photographic reproduction of an "ideal" copy of the First Folio of Shakespeare; Hinman attempts to represent each page in its most fully corrected state.

Key to Famous Lines and Phrases

If music be the food of love, play on.　　[*Orsino*—1.1.1]

And what should I do in Illyria?　　[*Viola*—1.2.3]

O, you are sick of self-love, Malvolio, and taste with a distempered appetite.　　[*Olivia*—1.5.89–90]

Make me a willow cabin at your gate
And call upon my soul within the house,
Write loyal cantons of contemnèd love
And sing them loud even in the dead of night . . .
　　　　　　　　　[*Viola*—1.5.271–74]

. . . she bore a mind that envy could not but call fair.
　　　　　　　　　[*Sebastian*—2.1.28–29]

O Time, thou must untangle this, not I.
It is too hard a knot for me t' untie!
　　　　　　　　　[*Viola*—2.2.40–41]

Not to be abed after midnight is to be up betimes . . .
　　　　　　　　　[*Toby*—2.3.1–2]

O mistress mine, where are you roaming . . .
　　　　　　　　　[*Fool*—2.3.40]

Am not I consanguineous?　　[*Toby*—2.3.78]

Dost thou think, because thou art virtuous, there shall be no more cakes and ale?　　[*Toby*—2.3.114–15]

221

I have no exquisite reason for 't, but I have reason
good enough. [*Andrew*—2.3.143–44]

The spinsters and the knitters in the sun
And the free maids that weave their thread with bones
Do use to chant it. [*Orsino*—2.4.50–53]

Come away, come away, death . . .
[*Fool*—2.4.58]

She never told her love,
But let concealment, like a worm i' th' bud,
Feed on her damask cheek. [*Viola*—2.4.122–24]

. . . like Patience on a monument . . . [*Viola*—2.4.126]

Some are born great, some achieve greatness, and
some have greatness thrust upon 'em.
[*Malvolio*—2.5.149–50]

When that I was and a little tiny boy . . .
[*Fool*—5.1.412]